Anonymous

Historical Discourse and Addresses Delivered at the 175th Anniversary

of the Reformed Church, Readington, N.J., October 17, 1894

Anonymous

Historical Discourse and Addresses Delivered at the 175th Anniversary
of the Reformed Church, Readington, N.J., October 17, 1894

ISBN/EAN: 9783337298357

Printed in Europe, USA, Canada, Australia, Japan

Cover: Foto ©ninafisch / pixelio.de

More available books at **www.hansebooks.com**

1719 - 1894.

HISTORICAL DISCOURSE

AND ADDRESSES

—DELIVERED AT THE—

175th Anniversary

OF THE REFORMED CHURCH,

READINGTON, N. J.

October 17th, 1894.

Press of
The Unionist-Gazette Association,
Somerville, N. J.

Prefatory Note.

Two things have impelled us to the preparation and publication of this little volume. One is the very unanimous expression that such a volume ought to be issued which was given by our many friends on our anniversary day. The other is the deep conviction —a conviction which has grown deeper with each day that has succeeded the anniversary—that a considerable amount of material was being brought together at this time which would undoubtedly be of great value to posterity. Some facts have been ascertained which might, a few years hence, be entirely lost. Hence we have felt the need of gathering them up at this time in some permanent form. We trust that their publication may serve to recall to many for a long time to come, the memory of an exceedingly pleasant day ; and that, in years to come, those who follow us in this " field which the Lord hath blessed" may find this volume a help to them in their endeavors to discern the way by which the Lord hath long led his people here. One thing especially, we think, will add interest to these pages, viz. : the numerous cuts of church buildings and pastors which have been brought together and published for the first time. For the drawings of the two earliest church buildings we are indebted to one of our church's skillful sons, Mr. Ira Voorhees, of Somerville, N. J. The third is the workmanship of Mr. Andrew Hageman, now of Illinois.

With the earnest desire that these pages may serve to enshrine " Old Readington" more than ever before in the affectionate remembrance of all our children and friends, and also that their record may inspire those who still abide under her shadow to renewed consecration of themselves to Zion's grand work, we leave them with the public. On behalf of the Consistory.

        B. V. D. WYCKOFF,
        JOHN FLEMING,   } Committee.
        SOLOMON ROCKAFELLOW.

Anniversary Exercises.

MORNING SESSION.

Wednesday, October 17, was a day long to be remembered by the congregation and friends of the Reformed Church of Readington. That day had been selected by this church as the date for the celebration of the 175th anniversary of its existence. Fairer skies, balmier air, and conditions more delightful in every way it would have been impossible to provide. Providence had smiled most brightly on their undertaking. Hosts of friends from all directions gathered on the church grounds at an early hour, and when the time for opening the services arrived every tie-post within reach of the sanctuary was taken, and the pews of the capacious edifice were full almost to overflowing. The exercises commenced at 10:30 o'clock. The choir sang an appropriate anthem, after which the 103d Psalm was read by the Rev. W. H. De Hart, of Raritan, and then an eminently appropriate prayer was offered by the Rev. George S. Mott, D. D., of Flemington, who also annouunced hymn 149. After the singing a historical discourse was delivered by the pastor of the church.

Historical Discourse by the Rev. B. V. D. Wyckoff.

PSALM 77, 10, 11—"I will remember the years of the right hand of the Most High. I will remember the works of the Lord: surely I will remember Thy wonders of old."

I have selected these words as the basis of my discourse this morning because they express exactly the idea that I have had, and that I think this people has had, in arranging for this celebration. So far as we know, Readington Church has never hitherto celebrated an anniversary of this sort. We have thought therefore, that it might be wise for us at this time to pass in review these many years of our church's life and work. Such a review can hardly fail to increase our acquaintance with and respect for our long and honorable past—while at the same time we trust that it may arouse in us new gratitude and a more loving allegiance to Him from whose hand these years and their accompanying blessings have come.

I may state at the outset that I do not expect to lead you along any new and unexplored paths this morning.

It is not for me to blaze a way through any hitherto untrodden wilderness. Many as are our church's years, and far back as she reaches in her influence over this community and others around it, her entire life has been traced out and very accurately set forth by at least two writers who had access to all the facts, and whose books are procurable by all.

One of these was the Rev. Dr. Messler, in whose "Historical Notes," published in 1873, we have a brief but very complete sketch of our past. The other was that beloved son of this church, now made "perfect through sufferings," the Rev. Henry P. Thompson, whose "History of Readington Church," issued in 1882, gives an exhaustive recital of the facts and brings the story down almost to the present day. From this you will see that the task which falls to my lot to-day is simply to glean from these and from whatever other sources may be open to me, that which shall suffice to set before your minds with some degree of distinctness, for the purposes of the present occasion, these one hundred and seventy-five years and their manifold mercies. That purpose will be best attained, I think, if I ask your attention to two things:

First, the times out of which this church arose; second, her one hundred and seventy-five years of work. First then let us consider

I. THE TIMES OUT OF WHICH THIS CHURCH AROSE.

As we are observing our one hundred and seventy-fifth anniversary to-day, it would be entirely natural to suppose that we were one hundred and seventy-five years old. In reality, however, we consider ourselves somewhat older than that.

This church is so unfortunate as not to know the precise day, or even the year, of her birth. All that we know certainly of her earliest history is that the first church edifice, which was begun in 1718, was completed and taken possession of in 1719, one hundred and seventy-five years ago. That edifice stood on the brow of the hill overlooking the junction of the North and South branches of the Raritan, almost in front of the present residence of John Vosseller. That church was known as the "Church *over* the North Branch," and later as the "Church *of* the North Branch," because of the fact of its overlooking that stream. It remained till 1737, when, tradition says, it was destroyed by fire; and when the congregation came to rebuild, they moved farther West, and reared their new house of worship very nearly on the site of the present structure, where, because of its being within the bounds of Readington township, it grew later to be known as the "Church of Readington." I stated that that first edifice was begun in 1718. That, as you see, was one hundred and seventy-*six* years ago. It is hardly likely that that house would have been erected had there not been a congregation previously organized. Hence it is clear that our congregation must date back at least to 1718, and we cannot be sure that it did not exist even a year or two earlier. Dr. Messler, who carefully reviewed all the facts in the case, gave it as his opinion that there certainly was a church organization here in 1718, and that it was altogether likely that it began earlier, possibly even as early as 1715. Hence we have ground for saying that we feel sure we are one hundred and seventy-*six* years old, we suspect we may be one hundred and seventy-*seven*, and it would not surprise us very much if—were all the facts known—we should be found to be even one hundred and seventy-*eight* or nine. I would like now to set before you briefly the conditions amid which this church had its birth. First, let us glance at

1. *The temporal surroundings of that newly-organized congregation.*

The first settlers came to this region about 1700. Less than twenty years, then, before the rearing of that "Church over the North Branch" the entire country about it was a wilderness.

Historians tell us that it was everywhere covered with dense forests. Through these there were no roads. The only openings that could be found anywhere were a few natural clearings in the lowlands along the rivers. These were cultivated somewhat by the savages, and so it came to pass that there was a trail from one patch to another, along the North bank of the Raritan, from the site of the present city of New Brunswick, to Bound Brook and Somerville, and so on to the head-waters of the river. That trail was the only road the first settler here had to the outer world, save as he put his flat-boat on the waters of the Raritan, and allowed it to float downward with the current. Then, when he had discharged his cargo and wished to return home, he had to tow it laboriously all the way up-stream. To show you further the wildness of this country at that time, I may say that the History of Hunterdon County tells us that there was in those days an Indian settlement near the site of the present village of Centreville, and that when these Indians disposed of the principal part of their domains to the whites a few years later, they still reserved some land for themselves. That land now constitutes the farms owned by Backer Hoagland and John S. Craig, situated about two miles

FIRST CHURCH BUILDING,
ERECTED 1718-19. BURNT 1737.

Southwest of this church. It is difficult to conceive that we live so near to primeval times, is it not? Or rather, it is difficult to conceive that this church, which still seems so youthful and vigorous, has a life behind her which goes back so far into the past. But, from these temporal conditions let us turn to a survey of those that were spiritual.

2. *Spiritual surroundings.*

Until two days ago I had it in mind to state that I believed that that first church at the headwaters of the Raritan was the first distinctive house of worship erected anywhere in this region—in fact, anywhere between the old church at Three Mile Run, and the Delaware River. I do not mean by this that I thought it to be the oldest church organization. There were two church organizations in this territory before ours was established, viz.: The Church of Raritan (now First, Somerville), organized in 1699, and the Presbyterian Church of Bound Brook, organized in 1700. But though the dates of these organizations preceded ours, I failed to find that either of these congregations possessed a church building until several years after ours had been reared.

Dr. Messler says that the Raritan Church built its first edifice in 1721, and the "History of Somerset County" informs us that the one at Bound Brook was erected in 1725. From which facts it would appear as if until these dates, both of these congregations had been content to worship in convenient barns or other temporary quarters.

That would have made our first church building, for a number of years, the only thing of its kind in the greater part of this wide region that is now known to us as Somerset and Hunterdon counties. Two days ago, however, I was informed by the pastor of the First Church of Somerville that I must make cautious use of this statement, inasmuch as very recently it had been brought to his notice that there existed somewhere an ancient document, which, if it could only be secured and verified, might prove conclusively that the Church of Raritan had a "new church" as early as 1709. I trust that document may be found, and also that its records, when examined, may fully establish this very important fact. I am sure no one could rejoice more heartily than the daughter over the knowledge that her honored mother had been well housed and fully established ten years earlier than herself, especially as in this case the daughter would still have had a sufficiently wide field left her, a field that reached all the way from Roysfield to the Delaware river, and included some of Somerset and the whole of Hunterdon County. And then we must recollect how great a need that church supplied. The life of those early settlers must have been an extremely hard, toilsome one, affording scant time for the cultivation of religion except as it was determinedly snatched from the midst of most pressing duties. Morality was in a low state the world over. Infidelity had cast its blight over the fair lands of Europe, and its advocates were not slow in speeding its progress in these new lands beyond the sea. The Hollanders who came to this section were constitutionally far more religious than many of the emigrants of that day, but yet they were far from perfect. Above all else church privileges and ordinances had been up to this time about the scarcest things that could be found in all these parts.

About twice a year previous to 1720, good old Domine Bertholf, the pastor of all northern New Jersey and a considerable portion of New York, had made it his duty to visit this region, preach and administer the sacraments, and thus semi-annually had sought to blow the coals of spiritual life that he found here into renewed warmth. Those were the only spiritual advantages our forefathers in this region enjoyed up to the time of the founding of this church and the arrival of its first pastor in 1720. Can we not conceive somewhat of the joy that must have filled their hearts at the sight of the laying of its foundation stones? And when its completion was announced must there not have been a felt if not expressed cry of "Grace, grace unto it."

But we have dealt at sufficient length upon the beginnings. Let us turn our thoughts next to

II. THE ONE HUNDRED AND SEVENTY-FIVE YEARS OF WORK THAT HAVE PASSED SINCE THEN.

These years may, I think, be divided into two periods, the first of which is that of collegiate relationship with other churches, and the second that of independent organization. The former of these reaches from the date of the coming of the first pastor, in 1720, to the separation from the church of Bedminster, in 1800. These eighty years saw four full pastorates, and a portion of the fifth. The first of these pastors was that father of evangelical religion in these regions, the Rev. Theodorus Jacobus Frelinghuysen. He served Three Mile Run, (now First, New Brunswick, or Franklin Park), and Raritan, (First, Somerville), in connection with this church. His labors in this wide field must have been exceedingly arduous, but for twenty-seven years he continued them unceasingly. He met with bitterest opposition because he was so stern and uncompromising in his treatment of the sins of his day. But he kept fearlessly on his way, doing his divine work of giving utterance to the whole truth, whether men would hear, or whether they would forbear. The result proved his wisdom. Toward the close of his life he enjoyed greater quietness. Men came to appreciate better, no doubt, the solidity and permanence of his work; and to realize the advantage of building up the church on the grand foundations that he had so laboriously laid. During his pastorate, in the year 1737, the old log church overlooking the river burned, and the next year the second edifice was reared near where we are sitting, at the Southwest corner of our present church-yard, just back of the old locust trees that were removed a few years ago. That church was of somewhat peculiar construction. It was almost square, the longer side being the front and facing the road, while the roof slanted to the front and rear instead of to the sides. A drawing of this building may be seen yonder in the rear of the church, while a plan of its galleries, showing the position of the lofty pulpit at the rear of the house, may be seen in our ancient volume of minutes, where it was probably placed long years ago by some careful church Treasurer, and has remained ever since, being handed down from generation to generation with the most scrupulous care. It was my exceeding privilege, a few days ago, to stand beside the little plot in the old cemetery at Three Mile Run where lie the remains of Mr. Frelinghuysen.

Until a few years ago that spot was practically unmarked, and almost unknown. Now, however, by the timely and eminently appropriate act of some of those who bear his honored name, a plain but stately granite stone stands at the head of the narrow mound, precisely such a stone as one feels should mark the spot where rests one whose life was so strong and brave and enduring. I give herewith the simple but expressive inscription which that stone bears:

"Rev. Theodorus Jacobus Frelinghuysen. Born at Lingen, East Friesland, in 1691. In 1719 he was sent to take charge of the Reformed Churches here by the Classis of Amsterdam. He was a learned man, and a successful preacher. The field of his labors still bears fruit. He contended for a spiritual religion. "His motto was, 'Laudem non quaero, Culpam non timeo.'* He died in 1747, and his descendants, humbly sharing in his faith, have erected to his memory this monument."

Following the elder Frelinghuysen came his son John, whose

---

*"I seek not praise. I fear not blame."

pastorate was brief, reaching from 1750 to 1754. He was of a milder spirit than his father, and yet he was by no means lacking in either depth of conviction or firmness of character. During his pastorate the entire church was rent well nigh asunder by a furious struggle between the two parties that had been gradually forming in it, viz.: those desirous of forming an American Church, and those who were content to remain under the guidance of the mother Church in Holland. In this struggle John Frelinghuysen gave promise of being a principal leader and pacificator.

As it was he did much to bring peace to his beloved Zion, but ere he could accomplish all that it was his desire to do, he was unexpectedly removed by death. With his decease our connection with the Three-Mile Run Church ceased, that church deciding thenceforth to call a pastor of its own. Several years elapsed before Mr. Frelinghuysen's successor was found.

It was 1758 before the next pastor was settled. This was Jacob Rutzen Hardenberg, one of John Frelinghuysen's theological pupils, who also soon after married his widow and later occupied his house at Raritan, and so became in the fullest sense his successor. His pastorate covered the period of the War of Independence, which was a most trying time for religious effort.

Many churches in different parts of the land were compelled to cease their work altogether during these years. Dr. Hardenberg's field fared better than that, and yet evidences are not lacking that prove how greatly his work was hindered. One such evidence is the fact that this church possesses no records whatever of this pastorate. Our historians, when seeking light on the events of this period, have been compelled to resort to the records of the mother church in Somerville. One event of this time that is worthy of note was the removal of Queen's College for several years from the town of New Brunswick to the forks of the Raritan, by reason of the exigencies of war. For some time the college was sheltered here, continuing its work in the house formerly occupying the site of the present abode of John Vosseller. Another item of interest was the separation from the churches of Millstone and Neshanic in 1761, and from Raritan in 1781, the latter being the date of Mr. Hardenberg's removal to another field of labor. Two years after his departure Simeon Van Artsdaelen, a young man, became pastor here. His service, like that of John Frelinghuysen, was very brief, being terminated also like his by death, in 1786, after having wrought among this people only three years.

We can conceive that his death was viewed by his people as little less than a calamity, for he was a peculiarly lovable and eloquent man, devotedly attached to his work and people. During his short pastorate he received numerous and very flattering calls from other churches, but could not be induced to resign his work here. His grave is in our church-yard, with his wife's beside it, the first of the many that have since been occupied by ministers of the gospel who have had to do with this church.

The next pastorate was an epochal one. The Rev. Peter Studdiford came here in 1786, and remained forty years. For fourteen years he served Bedminster in connection with this church. Then, in 1800, that church withdrew. Thus Readington was left at last alone, and from this date commences her independent organization. But though alone, her field was by no means narrow. Dr. Studdiford lived near South Branch, on the farm now owned by his kinsman of the same name, Peter Studdiford, and his parish extended from Roysfield to the head of the Round Valley, and from the North Branch and Rockaway to Rowland's Mill and Mettler's Mill, on the South Branch. It was a wide field, requiring a vast amount of pastoral labor. Dr. Studdiford was lame, having had his knee injured by a musket in the hands of a British soldier, when he was a boy in New York, yet he faithfully served this people for forty years. When I came here, ten years ago, I heard some of our older people tell how clearly they could recollect the Doctor's horse and gig, with which he travelled everywhere, over rough and half-broken roads, and in and out of the almost unending lanes with their innumerable bars.

But besides being a thorough pastor, Dr. Studdiford was distinguished as a man of remarkable pulpit power, especially when called to speak impromptu. One who knew him well said that he was "one of the most efficient ministers of his day." It is pleasant to think that his work descended to his son, and then to his son's sons, one of whom, the Rev. Dr. Samuel M. Studdiford, still remains, proclaiming Christ most acceptably in the city of Trenton. During this pastorate two churches were organized from this one in some part, that of Rockaway being established in 1792, and that of North Branch in 1825, only one year before Dr. Studdiford's death.

And now we come to the pastorate which, all things being considered, may be called the most remarkable of all those that our church has enjoyed. It was that of the Rev. John Van Liew, who occupied this pulpit from 1827, to 1869, a period of more than forty-two years. Long as was the preceding pastorate, this exceeded it by more than two years. Moreover, it was remarkable in other respects. During Dr. Van Liew's time of service the church grew greatly. Population increased rapidly, and the resources of the people were greatly multiplied. Readington became widely known as a prosperous farming community, and in this prosperity the church shared. Two church edifices were erected under Dr. Van Liew's ministry. The first of these was built in 1833, only a few years after the commencement of his labors. The old church had stood through ninety-five years, having been repaired but once, about forty years before.

Besides it is probable that the growth of the congregation necessitated an enlarged building for their accommodation. The church which was erected at that time was placed on the spot occupied by the present building, the change of location adding somewhat to the stateliness of the structure, and also enlarging somewhat the church grounds. That church was destroyed by fire March 22, 1864,* after which the present edifice was erected. This building was dedicated July 20, 1865. A full account of the dedicatory services may be found in the "History of Readington Church," pp. 20-25. But in other than material things Dr. Van Liew's long pastorate was remarkable. As a preacher he was plain, practical and instructive. Were I to be compelled to characterize his pulpit work by a single word, I do not know that I could select a better one than this last—*instructive.*

He strove with all his power to mould into the very image of Christ this large household that God had entrusted to his care. But while he recognized faithful preaching as the first requisite to this end, he at the same time realized the tremendous influence of a godly life. And such a life he lived in the midst of this people year after year. Of him it may most truly be said:

> "The lore of Christ and His Apostles twelve
> He taught, but first he followed them himself."

And it is remarkable how deeply that life was impressed upon those who were reared under its influence.

Those were days of strong, spiritually-minded, and influential men and women. The pictures of some of them hang yonder at the rear of the church. Those who have been absent from these scenes for any time, and who have returned to enjoy the festivities of this joyous day with us, may take pleasure in looking once more upon these faces. One there is among them, of which we cannot help saying that we know that it would have afforded its owner the greatest pleasure to have been permitted to see this day, and

---

*March 24, some say.

REV. PETER STUDDIFORD,
FIFTH PASTOR, 1786-1826.

READINGTON REFORMED CHURCH.

share with us its enjoyments. Judge Thompson's life was one which was most closely identified with the life of this church. We know that he would have delighted in this Anniversary.

But he had "served his generation" long and well, and the time for his departure had fully come. Nearly a year ago he "breathed his spirit forth, and fell in his Redeemer's arms asleep." Others there were, besides Judge Thompson, who wrought here, and became veritable pillars in this house of God. And not a few had their lots cast elsewhere, but wherever they went, they at once became prominent in every good word and work.

In them Dr. Van Liew's light still shines in many places. I am glad indeed that through the thoughtful generosity of his children, this grand man is to live anew in the midst of this community throughout the years to come by means of the beautiful tablet to his memory which it will soon be our privilege to see unveiled.

I might add as I conclude this portion of my narrative that four churches were organized during this pastorate, all of which drew their first strength very largely from Readington. They were, of Reformed churches—Stanton (1833), South Branch (1850) and Three Bridges (1872). And there was one Methodist church, that of Centreville, organized in 1869.

The rest of my story might perhaps be called modern history. It deals with events that are so recent and people who are so well known that I do not feel called upon in the least to undertake their advocacy.

The Rev. John G. Van Slyke followed Dr. Van Liew in 1869. It had been our expectation that he would be here today to recall some of the events of his pastorate, but at the last moment a telegram came announcing his detention by reason of the death of a near relative.

Dr. Van Slyke did not remain here very long, but suffered himself to be enticed away the next year by a sister church, which had grown envious of Readington's prosperity and happiness under his leadership. He was here long enough though to greatly endear himself to many hearts and to establish for himself a wide reputation as an able and scholarly preacher; to prove also his helpful, healthful influence over the throngs of young people who then filled this church.

He was succeeded in 1871 by the Rev. John H. Smock, whose term of service, as you well know, was twelve and a half years. Mr. Smock was known not only in this community, but also in others on every side of it as a good preacher, a genial companion and a man of commanding influence in the defense of right. He was deservedly popular with all classes, but especially, I think, with the young. It is a matter of great regret to us that he is unable to be here to-day. A prior engagement, coupled with the precarious condition of his health, made his presence impossible.

We may be sure his heart is here, though his bodily presence is sadly missed from our company. Mr. Smock resigned this charge in October, 1883, and removed to Glen Head, L. I., where he still resides and continues his ministerial work. In April, 1884, the present pastor was installed, and he has sought to fill this place and perform its varied work ever since. All that he has to say for himself is that he has found the parsonage on the hill a very pleasant home, and the work that has come to him as its occupant a most delightful one in every respect. God has given us the utmost harmony in our work of these almost eleven years. He has also visited us richly with his grace. Thirty-two communion seasons have passed in that time, and but one of them has left no new names enrolled upon our church book. The total of communicants received in that time is 245, of which 152 came by confession of faith and 93 by certificates from other churches.

"The Lord hath done great things for us, whereof we are glad."

And now in conclusion, how difficult it is to survey the past as we have done this morning—so long a past, and one fraught with so great significance—without feeling a longing to be able to project one's vision onward into the future. Fifty, a hundred, a hundred and fifty, a hundred and seventy-five years of the past have swiftly passed before us.

The good deeds wrought, and the people who wrought them, have risen before us to be studied anew. We have found them interesting indeed. The Frelinghuysens, Hardenberg, Van Artsdaelen, Studdiford, and Van Liew, these all have lived and wrought and died, and of every one of them it may be said "their works do follow them."

But what of the years to come?

Fifty, a hundred, a hundred and seventy-five years from now, what shall the remainder of this story be?

The Scriptures tell us that there is one thing that ever remains. Men may die, the most enduring structures may crumble and fall, the purest renown even may pass out of earthly recollection, but the "word of God abideth forever." That word has been, we know, the essential thing in this church's past. We hold it as the essential thing to-day. We believe that it will ever be thus. And so it will come to pass that as that word goes on to its ever-increasing triumphs, this old and dearly-loved church will continually renew her youth, repeat her anniversary occasions, attract to herself larger and still larger renown, until at the last she shall be permitted to see the bright dawning of that day beautiful which her faithful career shall have done much to advance.

> "'Tis coming up the steps of time
>   And this old world is growing brighter;
> We may not see that dawn sublime,
>   Yet high hopes make the heart throb lighter;
> We may be sleeping in the ground,
>   When it awakes the world in wonder;

> But we have felt it gathering round,
>   And heard its voice in living thunder.
>   'Tis coming! Yes, 'tis coming!"

At the conclusion of the discourse the Rev. James Le Fevre, D.D., of Middlebush, announced hymn 249, which was heartily sung. It had been expected that the Rev. J. G. Van Slyke, D.D., of Kingston, N. Y., pastor of the church from 1869 to 1870, would next address the audience, but a telegram having been received announcing his inability to be present, the next thing on the programme was the presentation to the church, by the Hon. Jacob F. Randolph, on behalf of the family of the Rev. John Van Liew, D.D., of a tablet to their father's memroy.

Presentation Address by the Hon. Jacob F. Randolph.

A very pleasing part of the service this morning has been assigned to me. It is to communicate to you, the officers and members of this church and congregation, that the children of Dr. Van Liew—his two sons and one daughter—who are here to-day, mindful of their childhood and youth so happily spent here in your midst, and not forgetting the very many kindnesses received from all the members of the congregation and remembering the earnest zeal of their father in his work as pastor of this church, desire to present to you the tablet yonder upon the wall, and to ask your acceptance of it. They do not present it for its pecuniary value, for that is only a trifle, neither for its beauty, for we see what has more beauty every day.

Upon the tablet is written:

IN MEMORY OF
REV. JOHN VAN LIEW, D. D.
BORN 1798. DIED 1869.
PASTOR, 1827–1869.

REV. JOHN VAN LIEW, D. D.,
SIXTH PASTOR, 1827-1869.

Which records the long years of active service for the Master, and we trust the passerby, as he reads the inscription, may be reminded of a well ordered Christian life, and be led thereby heavenward.

It is just a quarter of a century to-morrow since Dr. Van Liew was called away, and his end was peace.

In yonder cemetery his mortal remains are buried, awaiting the resurrection of the just. The plot, with its strong iron enclosure, and the beautiful monument upon it, are a tribute of his love and loving parishioners of this church.

A part of the inscription upon the monument is:

> "Living, we loved him;
> Dead, we revere him.
> Glorified, we shall meet him
> In the heavenly world."

In the heavenly world! The heavenly world! It is no flight of fancy; it is our own faith, which oversteps the grave and sees him there, watching with earnest eye one and another and another and still another and another of his parishioners here as they enter there, sealed with the testimony of this earthly Zion, that "this man was born in her," thus adding another and another and still another "Star to his crown of rejoicing."

At the conclusion of Mr. Randolph's address the tablet was unveiled by the Rev. Elias W. Thompson. It is a neat slab of the finest Italian marble, 18–30 inches in size, the inscription being in letters of gold. It is placed on the wall to the left of the pulpit, nearly over the pew occupied by the elders of the church.

In receiving the gift for the church the pastor responded with a few words of heartfelt gratitude to those who had so thoughtfully and lovingly sought to perpetuate in this sacred spot the memory of one to whom this community owed so much. At the conclusion of his remarks the Rev. E. W. Thompson made an announce-

22   ANNIVERSARY EXERCISES.

ment of the long list of relics and antiquities which had been brought together for this occasion, and were on exhibition at the front of the church; and invited all who were interested in such things to inspect them at their leisure during the day. (For a list of these things, see Note, at the end of this volume).

In the roomy basement beneath the church five long tables, capable of seating 238 persons at once, had been prepared. Thither the guests were invited and asked to partake of the bounty of the church. These tables were filled four times. Hence it is safe to say that 850 persons in all had the needs of the inner man supplied. Much pleasure was realized in the reunion of friends long-separated, and the two hours of intermission passed almost ere the people were aware of its flight.

AFTERNOON SESSION.

At 2:30 o'clock the congregation again assembled. The audience room was so crowded at that time that the aisles were filled with benches, and still many had to stand. The exercises were opened with the singing of an anthem by the choir, after which prayer was offered by the Rev. E. G. Read, of Somerville, and hymn 20, was announced by the Rev. J. B. Drury, D.D., editor of the "Christian Intelligencer." Addresses were next delivered by the pastors of the five churches once collegiate with this.: First, Raritan; First, New Brunswick; Millstone; Neshanic and Bedminster. These addresses are here published in the order in which they were delivered.

Address by the Rev. Wm. Stockton Cranmer.

I am reminded before I begin that I must be brief. Not only does the pastor of the church delicately hint that of making many words there must sometime be an end; but the very program itself, with its wealth of promise for the afternoon and evening, as well as the smiling presence of the pastors of many other churches anxious in their turn to greet you, urge me to waive the ministerial privilege of speaking for a full half hour.

For these are not the good old times when the all-day session was the regular, not the special order—when, between the morning and afternoon service the people assembled, not in the basement of the church for a railroad luncheon, but under the shelter of the white-topped farm wagons for the more leisurely if not more substantial fare. And when, polemics and dogmatics having been generously treated of while the sands in the pulpit hour-glass had slowly slidden through, the preacher would certainly turn it over again and invite the congregation to *have another glass*. " Domine," said a long suffering elder the other day, "I wish you would preach shorter sermons." " Shorter sermons! Why, I feel that I ought to give the people the sincere milk of the Word." " That's all right," said the elder—"the sincere milk of the Word, but these are the days of *condensed milk*."

Which is only another way of reaffirming that the good old days *are* gone. No more the toilsome assembling of the heavy farm wagons with their loads of coatless men and barefoot children ; no more the stands out there on the church-green where the slaves sold malt beer, crullers and gingerbread ; no more the stately and solemn entrance of Frelinghuysen, prince of pioneers, or of Hardenberg with the juvrouw on his arm, while the congregation waited standing until the good man had ascended to the pulpit and looked down benignantly upon them.

There were giants in those days—men of robust, sinewy faith, of sober speech and earnest life and religious convictions, intense and burning.

But that is not to say that those of these days are degenerate, and that the sons are unworthy of their sires. True we cannot still detect the wiles of the devil by the cut of a coat, nor hear the lures of the evil one in the scraping of a fiddle; but one has only to listen to such speech as we heard this morning to know that the succession is safe; one needs only to remember that for 175 years the call to repentance has sounded from this pulpit, and that the fruitage of six generations of church going is to be found in those godly men and women of this day who are the living incarnation of pious ancestral influence. Here flows still the milk and honey of the Gospel. Here the grapes of Eschol still ripen for the faithful and the brave. The land so laboriously won by the fathers is transmitted to you improved and enlarged, with opportunities and responsibilities correspondingly enlarged. That you stand ready to assume these responsibilities, anxious and able to do for the future what the past has done for you, I cannot doubt. Love to Christ is in every heart-beat; loyalty to His Church is a part of your daily thought. Others have spoken (and will yet speak) out of the experience of what their eyes have seen and their ears heard; me you will permit, as the latest comer into this garden of the Dutch Church, to look forward rather than backward, and to require of you in the days to come the realization of all this promise and potency of the past.

I have not known you hitherto. So far as I know, not a drop of Dutch blood flows in my veins. I am a sort of wild olive, grafted in. I am not a Dutchman, but I am a Jerseyman; I am not a Dutchman, but I am a Christian; and there's not a drop of blood of any kind but rejoices in your joy this day and thrills sympathetically with every appeal to local remembrance and ancestral pride. The old mother church of the Raritan Dutch, here present in my person to-day, brings you greeting. We are of one stock, one blood, one faith, one hope. The hope that flows so rejoicingly in you is of the same current that swells in us. Old

SECOND CHURCH BUILDING, 1738-1833.

you are indeed, and full of works, but not too old nor too affluent to receive what I bring you—the mother's blessing.

It was a graceful word that your pastor spoke concerning our search for the date of that old first building. When the date (1709) shall have been proven, we shall have recovered a fact of local church history unknown to Dr. Messler, and gotten us a house of worship ten years before our proud and prosperous daughter took up her home in the famous log church over there at the head waters of the river. Indirectly this is already proved, one might say, by the fact that the first elders and deacons of the Readington Church had their children baptized in the Raritan Church, and that some of those same children, baptized before the time of your organization, afterwards became your honored office bearers. If the Raritan congregation worshipped in a barn or private house, the inference is that you, too, might have done the same and need not have gone so far for the sacraments. But you preferred to wait until, like the mother church, you could have your own house of worship.

In a few years now we, too, shall celebrate an anniversary—our two hundredth—and it may be that at that time we shall be in a position to make the occasion memorable in some such fashion as you have done this day, by the unveiling of a tablet and the utterance of feeling tribute to the memory of one of God's faithful servants. Meantime it is pleasant to be reminded that the grave of him who served us jointly for so long a time, the first (and may I not say the saintliest) of them all is neither lost nor neglected as we feared. Your pastor has read the inscription on the monument erected over that grave, the grave of Theodorus Jacobus Frelinghuysen. And in two things only has your pastor erred: first, in not giving me credit for having called that important matter to his attention; and second, in not translating for us the Latin motto. I asked one of the more learned brethren to give me the sense of it, and he says it means, "I ask not favour, I fear not blame." Lofty soul! Of such stuff and fibre God's prophets are made. May that "spiritual religion" for which he contended, that gospel of the grace of God in the heart, long continue to be the glory of this pulpit, and the unfailing comfort of your lives! Never may there cease to be heard in this place the old-time protest against formalism in the churches; and never may there fail to be made, of those who would enter the Kingdom, the old-time, the all-time requirement, "Ye must be born again!"

And now, what can I better do than give you the ancient salutation of the Dutchman as he went from house to house at the beginning of the year:

> "Long may you live!
> Much may you give!
> Happy may you die,
> And Heaven be yours
> By and by!"

Greetings of the First Reformed Church of New Brunswick, by the Rev. P. Theodore Pockman, Pastor.

My Dear Bros. and Friends:—The First Reformed Church of New Brunswick brings greetings to her sister at Readington. The pastor, consistory, members, and even the children unite in this salutation. We rejoice in your age, your strength, your promise of continued usefulness. It is not my purpose to draw historical items from the archives of our church to mingle with such as you have already listened to lest I should produce confusion in your minds. You want to keep the dates and facts of your own history clearly before you. Permit me, however, to say briefly that we celebrated our 175th anniversary two years ago last Spring—April, 1892. We have two or three more gray hairs in our head than you have. We are sure that we are as old as that for our consistorial records commence with the date of April 12, 1717, and our Baptismal record is complete from that date to the present time. There can be little doubt that there was preaching at the Raritan river where our city now stands as early as 1703, and it seems to be beyond question that our first church building was erected by 1714—three years before the formal organization of the church.

While reflecting upon the matter of our collegiate existence for many years there came to my mind the *parallelisms* in the life of our two churches, and of these I desire to speak.

1. In Church Buildings. Your first edifice was described as " broader than it was deep," etc. Our first house of worship has been portrayed as follows:

The church of the " River and Lawrence Brook " stood fronting the river. The structure was of wood, and, like most of the early churches, its breadth was greater than its depth. Its dimensions were 50 feet broad and 40 feet deep. There were seven pews on each side of the pulpit, and eight along the middle aisle. The total number of pews in the building was fifty and they accommodated about 300 persons.

When I first saw your *present* building I was struck with its similarity to ours. Yours is built of wood and ours of stone, but the general plan is the same. Your pews are arranged as ours, your galleries extend around three sides as ours, and the general impression of space and neatness and light are very much alike. Surely our ancestors were of one mind when deciding what style of building would be most suitable for the worship of the Triune God.

2. A second parallel is found in the fact that both congregations enjoyed the ministrations of the same ministers. Your first

pastor, Theodorus Jacobus Frelinghuysen, was our first pastor and during the same period of time from 1720 to 1748.

In the strictest sense we were then collegiate. During the next twenty-five years while you were served by two different pastors we were served by only one and the churches were independent, but your third pastor—Jacob Rutsen Hardenbergh—was afterwards our third pastor. Shortly after leaving you he came to New Brunswick to be the first President of Queens College and to be pastor of our church. He was one of the original trustees of Queens College. He brought to us the results of his labor and experience among you and we were blessed with the fruits of his maturer years. The traditions of his faithfulness and efficiency still live. His grave is with us to this day and his memory is blessed.

Our good fortune as sister churches was to have the ministrations of these great and good men. We were similarly instructed in doctrine and doubtless in matters of discipline were handled alike, although their method might not have been like the preacher in New York State many years ago who settled things in a summary fashion. Complaint was brought to him that an axe had been stolen and the parson, after listening to the statement, comforted the loser of the edged tool by saying he would find his axe. On the following Sunday the domine took two cobble stones into the pulpit and at a certain point in the service paused and related what had come to his knowledge about a stolen axe and "now," said he, "I propose to throw this stone (raising his hand as if to throw) at the person who took that axe." Just then a nervous wife grabbed her husband by the arm and exclaimed, "Dodge Jake or he'll hit you!" The parson needed only to add: "If you will call upon that man you may recover your axe."

Reference has been made to the esteem in which Dr. Hardenbergh was held here and to the deference shown Jufrow Hardenbergh. Well, I can assure you from what I know of our people one hundred years ago through their descendants, that we were not a whit behind you in these matters. If the whole congregation remained standing until the Dr. and his estimable wife passed up the aisle and she was seated, we did none the less in New Brunswick.

3. A third parallel lies in the fact that both our churches have been mothers of ministers and missionaries—around you are gathered your clerical sons to-day and in a far distant land your spiritual life has its representation.

Our dear old church has always nursed her children on the missionary idea and taught them the true missionary motive of *obedience* to Christ's great command; consequently the list of her sons that have entered the gospel ministry is a long one and the names of those who have gone into foreign fields (both men and women) are conspicuous; headed by no less a champion than David Abeel the pioneer missionary to Amoy, China.

4. Again our churches have had a similar experience in the way of *revivals*. Great seasons of refreshing have come to us time and again from the presence of the Lord. Only recently you had a thorough baptism of grace. It is recorded of Dr. Hardenbergh's ministry with us that it was almost a continuous revival—and the last four pastors have had experimental knowledge of the mighty power of God to bring many at one time to the feet of His dear Son. For these testimonials of the spirit's presence and power let us ever be thankful.

5. The last parallel of which I shall speak has to do with the present; and if I seem to be very personal you will grant me that the conditions warrant such reference. These two churches once collegiate, and always so similar in life and development, are now served by *two brothers*—two Dutchmen—to the manor born and bred.

Your pastor and I are sons of Dutch elders, were baptized in the Dutch Church, were classmates in grammar school, college and theological seminary, and have spent our whole ministerial lives in the Reformed Church in America. Early we were fed on the pap of Brown's Catechism, later on the milk of the Compendium, still later on the strong meat of the Heidelberg Catechism. We have subscribed to the doctrines of our church and preach them agreeably to the word of God, and if ever these two churches shall have itching ears and desire other forms of doctrine they will be obliged to seek them from other lips. We are bound by the traditions of the fathers in so far that we are determined to make our preaching as sound as theirs. If these close relationships do not make us twins, then no two mortals born of separate mothers can ever be twins. If these five parallels do not show that our congregations are essentially collegiate, still then no conditions other than those of being governed by the same body can establish such a claim.

My dear brother, I rejoice with you in all that this day means to you and to your people, and trust that you and I may be permitted to continue our ministry to such congregations until we shall have rounded out a goodly life and then exclaim with triumph in the last words of Dr. Hardenbergh: "I am going to cast my crown before the throne. Now I shall go to rest, for I shall go to be with the Lord. Hosanna!"

Address by the Rev. Theodore Shafer.

It gives me great pleasure; I count it an honor and esteem it a high privilege to stand here this afternoon. To me it appears like a family reunion. The brothers and sisters toiled, wrought faithfully together until they had gotten some substance, and then with true, characteristic, American independence started for themselves. They husbanded their resources until they were each able to care well and bountifully for their own. The strongest ties of love, fraternal intercourse and united effort bound them together as one church. All working under a common head, all striving to promote a common cause, all inspired and urged forward by a common master. They were not only one in name, principle and virtue, but one in the great struggle for wise establishment, for heathful growth, for true church independence. They then exemplified that never dying, never failing truth, the motto of our own beloved church, in union there is strength, courage, victory.

We are here to-day to enjoy the happiness, prosperity and hospitality of our elder sister. We lay with loving hearts and gentle hands our laurels at her feet, to-day we would crown her with the brightest of diadems. We can yet weep with you in your sorrows, yet bear with you your burdens, yet sing aloud with you in your time of happiness and praise.

We cannot forget that we were once co-laborers. This vast, beautiful, fertile domain belonged to us, and, as one man, together we cultivated our Master's vineyard. At that time our interests, our aims were identical; we fought bravely side by side for the development of Christ's Kingdom and the salvation of precious souls. Distance was no barrier, no obstacle to united effort. The few miles which intervene between Readington and Millstone were only a pleasant, enjoyable walk, to the sturdy dominie of colonial times. It is inspiring to think that our forefathers stood shoulder to shoulder in their labors of love, that they bore together the heat and burden of the day, that they were co-workmen with one another and laborers together with God. This was a union which distance could not sever, which time could not destroy, but heaven surely bless. We can rejoice to-day that we were co-witnesses with the Holy Spirit. Christ said, ye are my witnesses. Christ sent the spirit to bear witness. The spirit beareth witness with our spirits that we are the sons of God. And it is the spirit which beareth witness, because the spirit is truth. It is by the co-operation of the divine and the human, the spirit of the christian, that the world comes to a knowledge of Jesus Christ.

The Holy Spirit incarnates Himself in us. He was sent to us, not to the world. In the great plan of redemption, God the Spirit has His part and man has his. If we be but an instrument, let us be the best possible tool for the Master Workman. If we be but an humble witness, let us be clear, convincing, all powerful. If we be but a mirror, let us reflect with perfection the person, character and work of the Blessed Master. Thus by the help, presence and wisdom of the Holy Spirit we will do greater, grander, more glorious work in the future than in the past.

If what I have said be true, we were and are yet the actual representatives of Christ in this section of country. What solemn and high significance there is in this fact, that we, if we are truly regenerate, bear our Lord's name, "The Christ," "One Christ in heaven, another Christ on earth; one the head, the other the body." The Church is the body of Christ, Christ Himself. Does not all Scripture teach the oneness, the unity, the entire absorption of the disciple and the Master. We grow out of our old nature into the very Christ. Christ walks, talks, acts, lives on earth in and by us. What a responsibility was upon our early churches? What upon us? The work done in our respective neighborhoods testifies that we have not been "apostate and worldly and unconsecrated." This gathering here to-day is a living witness to the co-laboring, the co-witnessing, the perfect manifestation of the Father, Son and Holy Spirit, by the churches, the individual members, the body of Christ which stood in early years in collegiate relation. May our separation only tend to the enlargement of Christ's demand, the enriching of Christ people. My

THIRD CHURCH BUILDING,
ERECTED 1833. BURNT 1864.

brother, to you I bring the congratulations, the salutations, the heart of Old Millstone.

Address by the Rev. John Hart.

The Neshanic Church sends through me, its pastor, its sincere congratulations on this your 175th anniversary occasion. You have called us sister, but I leave it with you whether we are your sister or you our mother. The record of the Neshanic Church says that the "Consistory of the *Noord-Brens* Church," came over to Neshanic August 25, 1752, and organized a church for the convenience of those members who were "far away from the other churches where the preaching of the Gospel is ,and are debarred of sufficient opportunity to attend the means of grace." The Consistory appointed in this newly organized church were evidently of the membership of this church. Later a line for defining the bounds of the two congregations was agreed upon, and the Raritan river was made the boundary of division. The Neshanic Church can boast of more than the Readington Church in that it knows the date of its birth. It has a building also of which it is proud; the walls of which for 121 years have listened to the voice of praise and prayer and sermon. It can also rejoice in the ministry of Domines John Frelinghuysen and J. R. Hardenberg. Besides it has had Van Harlingen and Polhemus and Froeligh and Labagh and Smith and Ludlow.

There is a common work for our churches to do, dear brethren, for we are similarly situated, both being entirely in the country. We must take a firm stand for temperance and the honoring of the Sabbath day and attendance upon divine worship; three things the neglect of which we with others stand particularly exposed to. Faithful in our work, we shall receive the glorious reward awaiting faithful servants. Again, in the name of the Neshanic Church, I bid you God-speed.

NOTE.—The Rev. John Van Liew was born in the Neshanic congregation.

Bedminster Greeting—By Rev. Thomas Walker Jones.

To the pastor and members of this congregation, I bring the hearty greetings of the Reformed Church of Bedminster. In the inspiring historical sermon, to which we this morning listened, allusion was made to the fact that the Readington Church had not during its extended life, observed an anniversary. A history such as this church can boast of is certainly worthy of celebration. To look back over one hundred and seventy-five years of ecclesiastical life and effort is a rare event.

In domestic affairs it is befitting, on the one hand, that parents should study the welfare of their children. They should look forward to the coming years when their children, if properly trained, will be able to enjoy whatever they may do for their comfort and usefulness. And the children in turn, when they come to years of maturity, should never forget to look back and recall what their parents have done in their behalf. So in ecclesiastical economy. The fathers, laboring devotedly for the church's advancement, should realize the great fact that the coming generations will be able to profit from what they do in behalf of Zion. And never should the sons of the church prove recreant to the blessed heritage of Godly fidelity, influence and example that comes down from those that preceded them.

This is to you a day of retrospection and reminiscence. What a stretch into the past! Not far from two entire centuries. No less than five generations of religious toilers have here labored for the sacred cause of truth and righteousness. No wonder you are so enthusiastic to-day. It is your duty as well as your delight to hold in high esteem the deeds of those who planted and matured and guarded this Zion so that now she stands so prominent and powerful in this locality.

Bedminster and Readington have much in common in their respective histories. When you were thirty-nine years old we came into existence. We were not your daughter, but your sister, a twin sister I would say, were it not for our difference in age, inasmuch as for thirty-six years our churches had the same ministerial headship. Rev. J. R. Hardenberg, D.D., your third pastor, was our first minister. In those days church extension was carried on by the planting of new enterprises in unoccupied territory, more than by the colonizing feature. Localities were pre-empted, as it were, for the cause of Christ by far-seeing and devoted ministers who were able to anticipate the growth of population. What a wonderful activity and influence marked the pastorate of Dr. Hardenberg, who for twenty-three years did such excellent and efficient work in your church and ours. We wonder at the abundance of the labors undertaken and accomplished by this devoted man of God. Some persons undertake much, but accomplish little. No man can do two things at the same time, and do them well. Nevertheless a multitude of activities tend to the increased power and usefulness of that man who has learned to apply himself intently and intensely to one thing—throwing his whole soul therein—and as soon as that is accomplished take up another with equal devotedness of time and toil ; and when that is done, still another. Greatness of influence consists in the aggregate of tasks well performed. A minister's first duty is for the souls of men. To win and culture them requires tact as well as thought. Spiritual zeal should mark the true pastor. This is chief. He who is the servant of God is emphatically the servant of the people, for their present and eternal welfare. The man who does the most good to the souls of men is without doubt the best and greatest minister. To preach and pray and plan with the sublime purpose of saving souls is the high and holy task assigned to the ambassador of Christ. If a preacher has time and talent for other things pertaining to the prosperity of his fellow-men, without neglecting this peculiar business, so much the better.

Dr. Hardenberg was not only one of the greatest preachers of his day, but one of the most efficient champions of American independence in those serious and stormy Revolutionary times in which his pastorate existed. He was foremost and forceful in his advocacy of American freedom. He assisted in the formation of the Constitution of this State and otherwise aided in National affairs. His name stands among the highest on the pages of our denominational and national history. Subsequent to his remarkable pastorate, after a brief interval of official separation, we were jointly served for the period of thirteen years by the excellent and energetic Rev. Peter Studdiford. This preacher was specially noted for the force and finish and freshness of his extemporaneous addresses. Also for his consecration to the highest and broadest spiritual interests of his congregations.

In one other feature we have a similarity of experience. While age marks our history, a youthful spirit pervades our churches. That congregation is not to be congratulated that glories in its past achievements to the neglect of present activities. We revere best the memory of worthy ancestors by catching their spirit, copying their earnestness and carrying forward to still higher and larger attainments the noble work in which they were successfully engaged. This is evidently your spirit, as revealed in the scenes and sentiments of this grand celebration. Bedminster heartily clasps the hand of Readington to-day, with cordial congratulations respecting your brilliant past, and warmest wishes for a future equally bright.

At the conclusion of this admirable series of addresses the audience rose and sang hymn 429. Then the pastors of the churches that have grown out of Readington Church were announced. The churches that were thus represented were Rockaway, North Branch, South Branch and Three Bridges, and the addresses follow herewith in regular order.

Address by the Rev. B. C. Miller, Jr.

My Dear Brother—It is entirely unnecessary for me to reiterate the expression of the joy which is so general at being permitted to take part in your joy to-day, or even to express the love which the church which I represent bears as a daughter to this church as her mother.

Brother Wyckoff came over to our centennial two years ago and spoke upon a subject which I imposed upon him, "The Relation of a Mother Church to Her Daughter." He has now turned the tables upon me and imposed the topic, "The Daughter's Relation to Her Mother."

The daughter's relation to her mother—where shall we learn this? Not in nature, but in grace; not in observation, but in inspiration; not in reason, but in revelation. Nature, observation, reason—these may furnish illustrations of the relationship; but if we wish to discover what it is and something of what it implies, we must go to the Book. Looking into Scripture to find something to say on this occasion, I was reminded of Antioch, the daughter, and Jerusalem, the mother, and "the mother of us all." And, following the law of God's Holy Spirit, as indicated in the history of the doings of these churches, I find that the relation of a daughter church to a mother church is at least twofold.

It is first a relation of ready helpfulness in time of need. When they of Antioch heard that there were famine and suffering in the old mother church in Judea, it is written that "the disciples, every man according to his ability, determined to send relief unto the brethren that dwelt in Judea." And this is an indication of what should be perpetually recognized and felt and done by daughter churches respecting mother churches. I know that the Christian Church has forgotten or thinks she has outgrown this as she has forgotten or thinks she has outgrown many things in the Scripture. No doubt you have had your times of need; but I never heard of our people sending you aid in these times—*perhaps* because you never let us know of your needs. Whatever the reason, here stands the revealed indication that the relation of a daughter church to a mother church is a relation of ready helpfulness. As no man liveth unto himself, so no church liveth unto herself. The shield of faith is never for selfish use; it is for the protection and aid of others also. O for a little of the tactics and discipline of the old Roman soldier! Each one had a shield large enough to protect himself; but in certain emergencies the whole phalanx would raise their shields above their heads and, either somehow locking them together or holding them together by the strength of brawny arms, would build an impervious roof over each other—"testudo," they called it, a turtle,—and march on to tremendous execution.

Secondly, the relation of a daughter church to a mother church is a relation of ready submission in time of dispute. When dissension arose in Antioch, " The brethren appointed that Paul and Barnabas and certain others of them should go up to Jerusalem unto the apostles and elders about this question." Your daughter has had her disputes; but I never heard of any of them being submitted to her mother according to this inspired example. Unless our Christianity follow the lead of the Holy Spirit in these things as well as in those technically called spiritual things, it is lacking. Unless our religion reach down and touch the pocket and regulate all money matters according to this Holy Word, unless it be influential and practical within us and within our churches when there is a flash of anger in the eye, there is something wrong. It is easy to get together and say sweet and pretty words to one another; it sounds grand and noble and even pious to utter great things about God and His cause; but unless these words are backed up by Scriptural deeds along the lines and on the planes which men—too many of even Christian men—are inclined to call low, they are but "sounding brass and a tinkling cymbal." It is on the so-called "low" planes that the reality of Christianity is seen and felt and proved.

These, at least, are implied in the relation of a daughter church to a mother church—ready helpfulness in time of need and ready submission in time of dissension.

Now, why not *manifest* this relationship? We cannot do this without remembering it. And we ought to remember it at least annually. Not just once in a hundred and seventy-five years ought this to be called to mind and great celebration of speeches and feasting made over it. Why not at least once a year—the Lord's day nearest to the 12th of January, our birthday, would be a good time, as respects us—why not imitate this same Antioch when she became a mother, and send a delegation to the daughter churches "to see how they fare." Don't just come in and sit down so that the pastor shall say, "Hm! Some of the Readington people here, to-day!" and that be the end of it. But let us know you are coming, or at least that you are there, as a delegation, with questions to ask and greetings and counsel to give; and you will be recognized and treated well and sent away home with responses and with love (and I wish I dared say with money, if you had need). Why not have an annual home-coming for all the children? Not once in a hundred and seventy-five years, but once a year; not for celebration, but for sympathy and practical help. Keep the relationship before us, the relationship of churches

—church daughterhood and church motherhood! The pastors are all right along these lines of courtesy and fellowship. They exchange, they love and sympathize and help. The people pass back and forth as occasion offers. But I plead for church helpfulness and church submission, according to the Scriptures.

As a molecule in the body of your daughter church, and in her name, I wish you, mother, love and success.

Address of the Rev. P. M. Doolittle.

I come to-day, with the greetings of what I may call The Second Church of North Branch to the First Church of North Branch. To me, the theory of ecclesiastical genealogy is somewhat confused. All these old churches aspire to be known as "Mother Churches." For the third time, now, within a few years, my church has been claimed as a "daughter church;" and I hear that the time is not far away when we shall again be expected to do filial duty. It is no uncommon thing for a woman to have many daughters; my church seems to invert the order of nature, in being the child of many mothers.

I sincerely wish I could demonstrate this relationship with the Church of Readington. I think I can account for the previous connection of those who formed the Church of North Branch in 1825, with a single exception. That one may have come from Readington; giving you "the benefit of the doubt" in her case, we will claim her as the old-time link that joined us.

Waiving all this, we of North Branch, are your next door neighbors, and good friends always. In 1827, our consistory appointed a committee to confer with a committee from your church, for the purpose of establishing "a division line" between the two congregations. That committee, so far as I know, has not yet reported, and it is hardly to be expected that it ever will report. In fact we need no "division line;" if it were drawn, it would

REV. JOHN G. VAN SLYKE, D. D.,
SEVENTH PASTOR, 1869-1870.

present as marvellous an instance of zigzagging as you ever saw ; if there were a line fence between us, we would wish it made up entirely of gates—rather would tear it away, and burn up the rails. We rejoice in free coming and going. If any two congregations were ever more interpenetrated geographically, more interchanged as to pastoral and social courtesies, and transfer of members, and more intermarried, I should like you to tell me. May we long live and flourish, in mutual harmony and good neighborhood.

My acqaintance and interest in Readington Church have consisted largely along with my intercourse with her pastors. I must confess, notwithstanding all appearances to the contrary, having lived beside you more than thirty-eight years. I first met Domine Van Liew in 1852, and was a neighboring pastor from 1856 until his death. I knew him well. He was venerable, dignified, affable and kind to young men. He was so substantial, sincere and always himself that knowing him at all was knowing him wholly; known once, he was always known by his friends. In looking back I lose sight of the time marks in his course, and it seems as though I must have known him and this church identified with him, from the date of his settlement here as pastor. He was patient, faithful and laborious; confirmed in his theories and established in his modes, he yet had a certain progressiveness, which made him successful and acceptable to the end of his pastorate.

Then came Domine Van Slyke, who made impressions and exerted influences here which are operative to this day. He soon began looking around to see just how much of Readington was absolutely and permanently essential to his happiness ; and when he had settled the question he took her upon his arm and walked off. Some rather resented his leaving, and one old lady remarked, " Well, if Mr. Van Slyke leaves Readington now I think he'll be but a rolling stone." However he has rolled over but twice, and if he has gathered no moss, he has gathered what is better. He is a much *greater* man than when he left here; "may his shadow never grow less."

Domine Smock succeeded him, and his pastorate was of considerable length. Active, keen, racy and exercising his powers in various directions, his ministry was highly marked and memorable. I grieve as I notice his absence from this scene on account of declining health, and may God's strength be made perfect in his servant's weakness.

And here is Domine Wyckoff, your present pastor. When he entered upon this field, my heart went out to him and has not yet turned back from him. His acceptability with all is fully recognized. His influence with the young is happily evidenced in connection with Christian Endeavor work. He is satisfying to the older members of his charge—one of whom doubtless spoke for many others in saying, "We never expected to get another minister so much like Domine Van Liew." We pray for his long continuance here, with increasing faithfulness in the spiritual advantage of his people.

We have been looking back today and celebrating history. Let us not fail to look forward as well nor forget that this generation is *making history*. Sin, in whatever form the outcropping may be, is in all the ages essentially the same. The same old Satan is alive and as intently as ever at work. Sin and Satan are to be met and vanquished. The weapons of our warfare are the same, well proved, adequate. The same Jesus Christ lives and reigns, and He leads on to victory. The end is not problematical.

A hundred years from now every one of this huge assembly will have gone hence. Oh! that every one of you may then, being glorified, look down from supreme heights upon those who may then be congregated here to celebrate the 275th anniversary of this church. May your labors, divinely blessed, greatly contribute to making her more glorious in the future than in the past.

READINGTON REFORMED CHURCH. 43

Address by Rev. Isaac Sperling, South Branch.

Who has not heard of Readington Church? You may go to the far West and find many there who love it. You may go to the North and to the South—yes, you may visit the other side of the globe and find those to whom its name is very dear!

When but a little boy I learned about it; and have always thought of it as being an historic organization.

As an individual, mine is more than a passing and ordinary interest. For since the beginning of the present pastorate, that interest has been drawn here in an especial way; because the pastor is a friend of my childhood, and one whom I highly esteem.

Happy and grateful in so doing, I feel it to be a great honor to represent a church that may be looked upon as one that has largely grown out of this.

It seems to me that Pastor Wyckoff must have had a feeling of awe and a sense somewhat akin to reverence as he undertook the task of going over those old sources of information which refer to the early history of this church.

How the strong characters of those who have gone before must have come back as he studied the old story!

How our attention was riveted and our hearts stirred as we listened to that grand recital this morning! O, the piety of the fathers of old!

The integrity, the faithfulness, the faith! How the blessed qualities all come back to us as we go over the meager records that refer to their church life and work!

Taking up our own record book, which to me is old, something of the same feeling comes as I go over the names of those recorded there as having brought their certificates from this church to unite in the new organization of Branchville.

Sixteen, if I mistake not, came at one time by letter, representing a strong faith and sturdy Christianity, to undertake the work as it opened up at South Branch in the year 1850.

Others also came who have since professed faith in Christ.

Early influences upon us have not been lost.

In that carefully prepared history, by one of the sons of this church, now of blessed memory, is recorded a statement by one who was among our first members. Said he to the historian: "I have seen the time in Readington Church when it was very easy to go to church on a week day, leaving hay in the field ready to 'come in'; and I have hoped I might see the same again before I die—and it looks very much like it now in Branchville."

We are a church-going people; for such was our early training.

I once heard reference made to a portion of a good Dutch congregation as being "the cream" of that congregation.

Now I want to say that "the cream" of the South Branch congregation is not collected all in one locality, but there is "cream" throughout.

Is it too much to say that the influence of this grand old church has contributed largely to such a state of affairs?

Ours is a peculiar relation, geographically. The old site of the first building is within our bounds.

The residence of the fifth pastor (Studdiford), was not far from our sanctuary.

Socially and spiritually, our relations are and have always been delightful.

At this time, there comes before my vision an aged mother in whose presence stands a devoted daughter. There cannot be heard the sound of human voice, as by look and gesture that daughter speaks to the one whom she loves so much.

For she has not the gift of audible speech, and therefore must say what she wishes to say in another way.

The relationship between that mother and daughter is an ideal one—so devoted to each other—no harsh or ruffled feelings, but a continuous flow of pure affection, and unceasing willingness on the part of each to do what they might for the other.

Now the Branchville Church through a humble representative brings greeting to Mother Readington this afternoon. And while she can give no eloquent testimonial of her esteem and gratitude in the way of an address, nevertheless there is all of the devotion and loyalty and fellowship that are experienced by the other members of the family.

To each of us it would seem as though we had all of what you have to give of interest and good will. But these funds are inexhaustible; and not one of your daughters will complain, because you do not show any preference or partiality, but make us all feel that we are very near to you.

What a joyous home-gathering this is! Truly your "children arise up" to-day and call you blessed!

We are not here to cast a cloud over the luster of this occasion, but we would, if possible, add to the brightness of this day by assuring you that to us you are not old. Those qualities and characteristics that endear you to us are by no means waning with the advancing years. One, among and with your children, ever setting before them an example of Christian faithfulness, fellowship and activity.

We are thankful, yea, we are proud, Dear Mother, that it is your life blood which flows through our veins.

May you continue to do the work the Lord has given you to do, even as you have done it in the past. And at last may it be ours to rejoice as one united church in the presence of Him who is the Great Head of the Church.

Address by the Rev. O. M. Voorhees.

In one of the earlier Psalms (the 15th), we find an answer to the question, "Who is a welcome guest in the house of God?" Among other characteristics this is included, "He that sweareth to his hurt and changeth not." Dr. Delitszh translated the passage thus:

"If he swear to his hurt, he changeth not."

And Dr. De Witt's rendering is, "He may swear to his harm, but he answers not."

The verse may be paraphrased thus: If he make a solemn promise or enter into a covenant, and it turn out to his disvantage, yet he swerves not from his promise, and as zealously fulfills the terms of the covenant as though it worked to his profit. He makes great sacrifices rather than break his word. This is one of the moral qualities demanded of accepted worshippers before God.

These qualities, as well as the others mentioned in the Psalm, should mark Christian organizations as well as Christian men and women, churches as well as church members. And if the church of Readington has exhibited the other characteristics required by the Psalmist as faithfully as she has the one to which I have referred, she must surely be accorded a royal welcome in the tabernacle of Jehovah and a dwelling place on His holy hill. And we may with confidence predict for her what the Psalmist affirms of the accepted worshiper, she "shall never be moved."

That this church has sworn to her hurt can easily be shown. There was a time when her spiritual oversight was acknowledged over a widely extended territory. Hers was a goodly heritage. The number of families reported was considerably over three hundred. On Sundays all these pews were occupied, the church was filled with worshipers and the congregation proud of its strength.

READINGTON REFORMED CHURCH. 47

But the church had sworn to be loyal to the Kingdom of God, and to make constant effort for the extension of that kingdom. The fulfillment of that promise required new organizations in other localities. But those organizations could not be formed and flourish if Readington held on to her members. To be true to her oath of loyalty to the kingdom she had to give up members, to suffer the loss of families, to witness a constant contraction and increasing weakness in her old age. She had sworn. It proved to be her trust. Yet she changed not. She swerved not from the obligations of her oath though she has suffered and still suffers in consequence. For her constancy let us give her due honor.

Of her loss in the formation of the other churches around, I have no positive knowledge. Their representatives have revealed so much as suited their purpose. But it remains for me to tell of her efforts and her loss in behalf of the most recently formed organization in this section, the church of Three Bridges.

For many years the pastor of this church had lectured statedly in the little school house on the corner, and a Sunday School was maintained there, largely through the efforts of Readington people. It is said that as early as 1863 an attempt was made to organize a church, but it failed on account of some misunderstanding as to the location of the church edifice. Ten years later, at the solicitation of a number of residents of the vicinity, the Committee on Church Extension of the Classis of Philadelphia, to which the Readington Church then belonged, held a conference with the people. Elder Joseph Thompson was a member of that committee. By a large vote (none opposing), the Classis of Philadelphia was petitioned to grant a church. A special meeting of the Classis was called, to meet at Three Bridges, at which the situation was thoroughly canvassed, and the church unanimously granted. This was June 20, 1873. A committee consisting of Revs. John H. Smock and M. N. Oliver, and Elder

Joseph Thompson was appointed, and directed to organize the church on Sunday, July 6. The committee met, received certificates of church membership; a consistory was chosen, ordained and installed, and the organization of the church declared complete.

These facts are set forth in a preface to the church register, and their truth attested by the signature of the chairman of the committee, who was then pastor of the church. There are, however, a few additional facts that I presume Pastor Smock did not feel at liberty to record. The thirty members that helped form the organization came from five churches, viz.: The Reformed Churches of Readington, South Branch, Neshanic, and Clover Hill, and the Presbyterian Church of Reaville. And of those thirty members, eighteen came from Readington; two more came before the first communion. Thus nearly two-thirds of our original membership came from this church and represent a loss of at least nine families. Nearly as many families have since come to us, so that Readington's loss in the organization of our church is about one-tenth the number of families now reported by her. She had sworn to her hurt yet changed not; so she surely merits our praise.

The relation between the two churches has ever been most cordial. As your church was foremost in helping organize ours, so you must needs have a friendly interest in us. Your former members have always been given a hearty welcome when on a visit to their old church home, and we trust that you have ever felt a home feeling when visiting us. The various pastors have found it convenient to exchange pulpits occasionally, and in many other ways a cordial, neighborly, Christian interest has been manifest. We rejoice to be so prosperous and handsome a daughter of so generous and lovely a mother.

We are still neighbors. And as it sometimes happens that the

REV. JOHN H. SMOCK,
EIGHTH PASTOR, 1871-1883.

daughter, married and set up at housekeeping for herself, finds it convenient to increase her stores from the generous abundance of the old house, so we shall not feel we are taking undue liberties if we now and then carry off and appropriate to ourselves a few choice morsels from the home larder. We have need of them, and we know you will not offer serious opposition. For though living apart we are of one family. Dropping the figures and stating facts, we find that several families living much nearer Three Bridges than Readington, still call this their church home. It is but natural to expect that in time these families or their successors will attend the church nearest them. It will be hard for you to give them up. But you have sworn, so you must not change. That would be going back on your record. We shall do our best to help them preserve the family likeness.

Do not think, however, that we are active proselyters, and that Readington is our special field of operation. More than once it has been said to me by your people: " We ought to attend your church. It is much nearer." My reply has been : "If you conclude to cast in your lot with us, we shall try and make you welcome. But we cannot urge you." As we believe the Holy Spirit was instrumental in making this church willing not only, but active also in founding the church of Three Bridges, so we believe He will direct those who come from you to us, and those also who return from us to you.

In conclusion, I wish to affirm my belief that for all her sacrifices in behalf of the Kingdom of God, the Readington Church will receive rich compensation. It will not come in a return of the old-time strength nor in less laborious conditions of church work, but in that satisfaction that accompanies work well done, and in the consciousness that her efforts have received the divine approval. She has and will continue to have not only the joy of her own ingatherings, but also a share in the harvests reaped from the fields she has helped prepare. We rejoice with her to-day in one hundred and seventy-five years of successful efforts and fruitful sacrifices, and bid her God-speed for the centuries that are beckoning her forward.

Hymn 235 was next sung, after which the pastor announced that letters of congratulation had been received from the following persons:

Rev. J. H. Smock, Glen Head, L. I.
Rev. E. W. Merritt, Salem, Conn.
Rev. H. P. Craig, Churchville, Pa.
Rev. D. B. Wyckoff, Ghent, N. Y.
Rev. C. E. Wyckoff, Brooklyn, N. Y.
Mrs. P. A. Studdiford, Lambertville, N. J.
Rev. H. D. Sassaman, Mount Pleasant, N. J.
Rev. Theodore F. Chambers, German Valley, N. J.
Rev. J. L. Stillwell, Bloomingburgh, N. Y.
Rev. R. W. Brokaw, Springfield, Mass.
Rev. I. P. Brokaw, D. D., Freehold, N. J.
Rev. A. V. V. Raymond, D. D., LL. D., President of Union College, Schenectady, N. Y.
Hon. Frederick Frelinghuysen, Newark, N. J.
Prof. H. A. Scomp, Oxford, Ga.*

The pastor then stated that Readington had one very near and dear neighbor who, owing to the fact of her having started as a German Reformed church, could not claim any special relationship, and yet he felt that the present occasion would be incomplete could we not have a few words from the pastor of the Reformed Church of Lebanon, the Rev. William E. Davis, who would make a "three-minute speech."

*The letter of Professor Scomp, who claims to be a son of this church, is so appropriate that we have decided to include it in our volume. It will be found at the end of the book.

Congratulations of the Church of Lebanon by her Pastor, William E. Davis.

When we see another honored and praise poured out from every quarter, it is very natural to wish to be able to claim relationship. Such is the feeling of the Church of Lebanon while the Church of Readington is being honored as she is to-day. But considering the fact that the Church of Lebanon was for many years a German Reformed church, we can hardly claim relationship. We must be content with acquaintanceship. This we do claim, and rejoice in it. Especially does the pastor of the Church of Lebanon rejoice in the happy feeling existing between these two churches. The three pastors of the Church of Readington, viz., Van Slyke, Smock and Wyckoff, have been and are to-day my much esteemed brethren. It is therefore a privilege for me to bring the congratulations of the Church of Lebanon to this old historic church. This we do, and our congratulations are as hearty as words and feeling can make them. We are citizens of no mean country, we think. Ours is a land better in our estimation than the Promised Land, for that was a land flowing with milk and honey, but ours with peaches and cream. And our congratulations to you to-day are just as rich as the products of our soil. Our church has lately celebrated her one hundred and fiftieth antieth anniversary—you to-day your one hundred and seventy-fifth. You being our senior, we make our best bow and bid you God-speed.

At the conclusion of Mr. Davis' words Hymn 330 was sung, and the audience was dismissed with the benediction by the Rev. O. M. Voorhees.

At 5:30 o'clock the friends gathered once more in the basement, and had their bodily wants again supplied.

It was estimated that about 450 persons partook of the evening meal, which was finished in time for the opening of the evening session.

EVENING SESSION.

At 7:30 o'clock the church was once more filled with the people present, and benches were again placed in the aisles and filled. The choir sang an especially beautiful anthem at the opening. The Scriptures were read and prayer was offered by the Rev. A. Paige Peeke, of Millstone. Hymn 107 was sung, and then the ministerial sons of the church were heard in the following order: Rev. J. B. Thompson, D.D., Andrew Hageman, Gilbert Lane, Herman Hageman, Elias W. Thompson and Jacob A. Craig.

Readington Negroes.—Address by Rev. John Bodine Thompson, D. D.

In commencing the early history of this church we ought not to forget its members of African descent. Some of them have been most godly and devoted Christians.

Berkeley and Carteret, the proprietors of New Jersey from its conquest by the British in 1664, "offered a bounty of seventy-five acres of land for the importation of each able slave."

But slavery in New Jersey was not so bitter as it was elsewhere. As early as 1694, trial by jury was secured to slaves here. "In every other colony in North America the negro was denied the right of trial by jury * * * but here in New Jersey the only example of justice was shown toward the negro in North America. Trial by jury implied the right to be sworn, and give competent testimony. It had much to do toward elevating the character of the negro in New Jersey * * * They received better treatment here than in any other colony in the country."*

*Williams' History of the Negro Race in America. He gives the cen-

READINGTON REFORMED CHURCH.

The first slave received into the communion of this church was "Black Tony, belonging to the Rev. Simeon Van Artsdaelen," pastor of the church; and others followed until slavery became extinct in New Jersey by virtue of the act passed February 24, 1820, which provided that children of slaves born after the 4th of July, 1804, should be free; if males, at 25; if females, at 21 years of age.

These temporary slaves, like the slaves for life, were sometimes hired out by their masters. Some of us here can remember our schoolmate, Richard L. Stryker, who had thus been hired by Domine Van Liew from the widow of his predecessor, Rev. Peter Studdiford. Afterward he became a prominent merchant in Liberia, and wrote from thence valuable letters of advice to the New Jersey colonization society. Once he came back to visit his friends here. He married a daughter of Governor Roberts, of Liberia, and amassed a fortune, which he left to his family.

Some of us remember, also, the Rev. Peter Miller, who, though not a member of this church, was well known in this community and frequently preached to congregations gathered in private houses in different parts of this congregation.

At one time slaves were regarded as real estate and their purchase and sale were conducted with the same forms as the transfer of land. But afterward they were regarded rather as personal property and were transferred from one master to another simply by bill of sale.

Here in this portfolio of mementoes prepared for this occasion are records of the purchase and sale of slaves in both these forms, which alike sound strange to modern ears.

In some instances the purchasers bought also the household

sus of slaves in New Jersey to the middle of the century, as follows: In 1715, 1,500; in 1735, 3,981; in 1745, 4,606; in 1775, 7,600; in 1800, 12,422; in 1810, 10,851; in 1820, 7,557; in 1830, 2,254; in 1840, 674; in 1850, 236.

stuff which the slaves were accustomed to use, in order that they might not seem to have their old homes entirely broken up. I will read the record of such a purchase by Abraham Post, the revolutionary soldier, who sleeps in the adjoining church yard after a stormy life of nearly a hundred years :

"Know all men by these presents that I, William Post, of Hillsborough township, in the county of Somerset and State of New Jersey, yeoman, for and in consideration of the sum of fifty-five pounds, lawful money of said State, to me in hand paid, by Abraham Post, of Bridgewater township, in the county of Somerset and State of New Jersey aforesaid, yeoman, the receipt whereof I do hereby acknowledge, having bargained and sold, and by these presents do bargain and sell unto the said Abraham Post, a negro wench named Eve and her child, a negro boy named Frank, and various kinds of household furniture, as bed, bedding, pewter ware, wooden ware, linen and yarn, and all and every other article or articles in her care and possession ; to have and to hold, all and singular, said wench and boy and goods and implements of household and every of them ; unto the said Abraham Post, his executors, administrators and assigns forever, and the said William Post, for himself, his heirs, executors and administrators, all and singular, said wench and boy and household stuff and unto the said Abraham Post, his executors, administrators, and assigns, shall and will warrant and for ever defend by these presents. In witness whereof I have hereunto set my hand and seal this second day of February in the year of our Lord one thousand seven hundred and eighty-five.

Sealed and delivered
in the presence of   WILLIAM POST. {L. S.}
DOUWE DITMARS,
HENRY POST.

Probably, this William Post was Abraham Post's nephew ; and the witness, Henry Post, his father, the brother of Abraham Post.

This same Abraham Post was sued by Minna Dubois (who also had been a soldier during the Revolutionary War), for the value of a slave and was compelled to pay him between $100 and $200. I do not know the precise nature of the offense ; but I believe that it consisted in refusing to separate husband and wife by driving from his premises one who was legally the slave of Minna Dubois. Dubois' attorney was Frederick Frelinghuysen, the grandson of the first pastor, and the son of the second pastor, of this church. His receipt for the value of the slave and the costs of the suit, as well as Abraham Post's memorandum of his expenses in defending it, are in this portfolio.

Some of us still remember "Dick and Rose" and "Sam and Kate" who used to come back occasionally to the farm on which they had lived as slaves to visit their "Young Missy," as they called her, and to exchange reminiscences of earlier days, which brought tears of alternate joy and sorrow both to her eyes and to theirs. They always went away loaded with gifts.

On what was once the glebe of this church, the farm on which the pastor lived, a mile west of us, on the road to the Drie Hook is a graveyard, surrounded by a stone wall, and cared for by this church. In that yard has recently been placed a gravestone, taken from a neglected grave near White House Station. This stone bears the name of George Anderson. He lived and died on "The Ridge," on the farm now owned by Mr. Henry Miller. In accordance with my suggestion the head stone was removed from the abandoned graveyard a few weeks ago, by the pious hands of George Anderson's grandson, Jacob G. Schomp, long time an elder of this church, and, though now eighty-eight years of age, present with us here in excellent health and spirits to do honor to this occasion.

George Anderson had a slave, who had been the slave of his father on his plantation near Raritan Landing, during the Revolutionary War, and had been the foster-mother of his children. From this fact she was known as "Old Maumy," which the irreverence of the third generation shortened into "Maum," and regarded as a proper *name*. Mr. Schomp still recollects the stories she used to tell of Cornwallis' dragoons, who passed her master's house on their raids from New Brunswick among the neighboring farmers. But they never molested her or her master (as she thought and said) because she was always so well prepared for them with pitchfork and ax and boiling water.

After the death of George Anderson on the Ridge, her *old* age found a refuge with his children, who cared for her as long as she lived.

When George Anderson's daughter, Mattie, married Captain Henry A. Post, her father gave her as a wedding present her maid, Phillis, of whom she was very fond, and who was equally fond of her. Phillis was efficient as lady's maid, seamstress and nurse; and was always and only a servant. But a brother of her new master, the husband of her young mistress, was a wild young man; and to save him from the consequence of a drunken frolic an entire corn-crop was sold. The consequence was that the next spring found the household in the most dreadful state of need; and, to raise money for present necessities, Phillis was sold, (I think to a man near Cranbury), with the express understanding, however, that she was to be bought back a year later at the same price.

As the end of the year drew nigh, her mistress worried about Phillis so much that her husband borrowed enough money from his neighbors to make up the price, and went after her. He did not return for many days; and explained his long absence by saying that Phillis had been resold to a man in Monmouth county. He had driven thither and found *her*.

But the tender and delicate woman had been compelled to work the whole season in the field; and had been whipped and beaten so that she could neither walk, nor stand, nor sit, nor even lie in an ordinary bed. She was permanently crooked and could do no work of any kind. But he had brought her on a specially prepared bed in his farm wagon.

Then he made for her a big cradle fitted to her deformity ; and in this she spent the remainder of her life, cared for by her mistress whom she loved. When she died, it was impossible to put the body into a coffin without breaking the legs. But this her mistress would not permit. Accordingly, a very large grave was made, and Phillis's cradle became her coffin. Her mistress's daughter, Ann, who had often rocked Phillis in her cradle, would sometimes tell the story of Phillis to her daughters [now Mrs. Aaron Hoffman and Mrs. Pierre Henri Bousquet] with a pity and pathos they can never forget.

The Dutch had possessions in Africa, as well as in North and South America, and slaves, as well as other merchandise were frequently transported from one of these colonies to the others. Those who came from the coast of Guinea were regarded as the most valuable, because of their superior endowments, both mental and physical. " Guinea negroes " brought more than others in the open market. Among these were a man who had been the chief of his tribe, with his wife, who now shared his slavery as she had shared his rule in the land of their fathers. These became the property of Jacob Kline, the grandfather of John Kline, the the well known elder of this church (who died nearly fifteen years ago at the age of 95). But slavery is bitter at the best, and it is no wonder that these Africans were fearfully homesick. Every endeavor was made to cheer and comfort them—save, of course, that of setting them free, which probably was never thought of. The result was, that when all hope was gone, they sought and found together the only freedom possible for them. The spot is still pointed out on Kline's brook, a mile directly north of this place, where stood the cedar tree upon which one morning the master found only the lifeless bodies of those who refused to remain slaves in a strange land.

I have a more cheerful story to tell of another Guinea negro, who attained his freedom I know not how. I hold in my hand a parchment deed, signed in a hand not accustomed to the use of the pen—"Aree Van Genee,"—*Aray from Guinea*, a name which the irreverent youngsters of a succeeding generation, punning upon the color of the man who bore it, travestied into "a raven Guinea!" I wish I knew his story in the land of his fathers; how he crossed the Atlantic, learned the Dutch language, obtained his freedom and became a wealthy and respected citizen. But of all this I am in entire ignorance. I know nothing of him earlier than the 3d day of April, 1730, when he purchased of Benjamin Rounsavall, carpenter, 132 acres of land at Potterstown, which was then within the bounds of this congregation. Ten years later (July 29, 1740), he sold this property to Matthias Sharpenstein. From this sale, however, he excepted two lots of about one acre each, which he no longer owned. One of these lots he had sold January 22, 1740, to William McKinney, and it is the deed for this lot which I hold in my hand. It is valuable chiefly because it describes the property as "beginning at a post for a corner standing in a line of land commonly called the West Jersey Society's land, it being a corner to *land layed out to the Lutheran Congregation Meeting House.*" I have also a deed for this Potterstown farm to Cornelius Wyckoff, executed May 11, 1761, by the children of Matthias Sharpenstein, excepting from the sale the "small lot formerly conveyed to William McKinney, and one other, *where the Lutheran Meeting House is now built.*"

These statements warrant the inference that the Lutheran Church at Potterstown (which afterward became the Reformed Church of Lebanon) was organized before 1740, and its edifice

READINGTON REFORMED CHURCH.

erected before 1761; and also that the land for the meeting house was given by this negro, Aray from Guinea.

After selling his property at Potterstown Aray bought land nearer this church, including the farm now in the possession of Mrs. Herman Hageman and the one back of it to Campbell's brook, on the banks of which he and his descendants lived and died.

His son, James Aray, was an honored soldier in the Revolutionary war; and his children were among the most respected citizens of this community within the memory of some here present. The first name of a free negro that I find upon the list of communicants of this church is Mary Aray. I believe that there are none of the family now resident here. Some of them have, I believe, been successful business men in New York city.

God makes even the wrath of man to praise Him. The man-stealers meant it for evil—and it *was* evil in them; but God meant it for good, that the inhabitants of the dark continent might learn the way of salvation and live the life and die the death of the righteous, loving and serving the Lord Jesus.

I have already alluded to Richard L. Stryker, who went from here to Liberia to do excellent work for the Master there. The records of the Somerset County Bible Society show a contribution made by negroes for the express purpose of sending Bibles to Africa. Heaven is vocal with praises from thousands thus redeemed from ignorance and sin. There is now looking out upon us from their heavenly windows "a great cloud of witnesses," including negroes as well as whites, rejoicing with us to-night in what has been done for the Master here in the days that are past, intent to see what we are doing for him now, anxious only that as our privileges are greater, so also our consecration shall be greater than was theirs. Shall their desires be realized? Shall we be better and do more for Christ than it was possible for them to do?

I append the names of the slaves and free negroes which I have found upon the records of this church, though the imperfection of the record does not allow it to be made complete:

Slave—Black Toney, belonging to the Rev. Simeon Van Artsdalen ; Sam, a negro servant of Peter Ten Eyck ; Martin Wyckoff, to be baptized ; Margaret, negro woman, of the widow Mauriceson ; William, negro servant of Joseph Van Doren ; Thomas, negro servant of Daniel Amerman ; Joseph, a negro man servant of John Wyckoff; Susannah, wife of the aforesaid Joseph, and woman servant of the aforesaid master ; ———, colored woman, wife of Sam. Hall ; Charles, colored man of Tunis Cole ; States, colored man of Cortland Voorhees : Dian, wife of States.

Free—Mary Aray, John Van Derveer, Susan Kline, Martha Schamp, Pompey Lane, Hannah Lane, Peter L. Kline, Elijah V. N. Ten Eyck, Margaret Ann Simpson, Sarah C. Lane, Josephine Dawes, Sarah C. Schureman, John Cox, Margaret Jane Lane, Leonora Condit, Charles Van Horn, James V. Van Horn.

Address by the Rev. Andrew Hageman.

I have been thinking to-day as to the exact reason why we sons of the church are summoned to respond. Possibly it is that we may give an account of ourselves, for here we still retain our church membership.

I have it to confess, that I have been married three times to churches. The first, a young bride born in 1858. The second, a bride older than my mother church, born in 1699. The last one, venerable also, born in 1700. I cannot decide which is preferable, the young or the old ; for I loved them all and they have each treated me right royally and handsomely.

I seem to be a connecting link in my ecclesiastical life of the scenes of the older laborers in the Dutch church in this State.

Bertholf, Morgan and Frelinghuysen were the first to serve our church in this State.

Bertholf was for twenty-four years stated supply at Belleville, my present charge. Morgan, for twenty-two years, served, as its first pastor, the Church of Middletown, now called Holmdel, my previous charge. Frelinghuysen, as we have heard this morning, for twenty-eight years was the first pastor of this church of my birth. I have thus been permitted to enter into their places of successful service.

As a son of this church, I therefore look back with pride to-night at her, and count it an honor to be one of her living sons.

I surely stand ready, in these closing hours of a most happy and memorable day in her history, to rise up and praise her for what she has done for me. Although she was more than a century and a half old when I was begotten of her into the grace of Jesus Christ, yet I realize the marks of her motherhood upon me.

The thought which I desire to emphasize in these few moments assigned to me is this: The power and influence of a church over the minister, born and grown up therein. In other words, I believe that the environment of our early years cling to us as ministers of the gospel throughout life.

This is a very comforting thought to me because I can look back to so much, which was pleasurable and profitable in those years of my life.

This is a most awfully solemn thought to me, as I look forward and realize the indelible influence of my life upon those, whom God has called or is calling in my own congregations into this most kingly of all services, the *Christian Ministry.*

And the life of each individual in every congregation has its influence, too, as such. "For no man liveth to himself."

I consider myself extremely fortunate in being born into this church just at the time I was. It was thirty-one years ago— nearly a generation ago. So what I say of praise is mostly concerning those whose work is almost or quite completed.

I am glad that the man of God, who received me as a lad of thirteen, so tenderly and lovingly into this church, has had his memory so conspicuously emphasized by this beautiful tablet unveiled this morning. It will ever greet the eye of those who worship here as an evidence of worthy esteem.

The impress of his life was left upon the generation of men who are almost gone. The parents of the most of these seven living sons of this church had their characters moulded and developed by this man of God; and we have entered in thus largely to the inheritance of their blessings.

The first thing which I will mention as stamped upon me by my early associations in this church is this. It may seem trivial, but to me it is real in illustrating the influence of early church associations.

I saw the old church consumed into ashes. From yonder seat of learning with a boy's vim I ran thither and watched it to the end. I recall the grave look upon the faces of the older men. I heard their resolves to build. I watched the progress until all was completed. And when I saw the effect of this so beautiful interior with its oak grain finish, I could conceive of no effect more beautiful and durable. And thirty years of wear upon it have proven that I was not a bad judge. What was the result? Just this. In my ministry I have built two chapels and remodeled a third; and somehow, minister like, I expressed my opinion and stuck to it, and to-day two of the three bear the marks of the oak grain.

Another thing stamped upon me by my early church associations here is this. I think it was largely born of the calm, dignified, gentle, loving, sympathetic manner of him who was my spiritual shepherd.

I never saw him impatient with his people. I learned a lesson for life. "That the servant of the Lord must not strive, but be gentle unto all men, apt to teach, patient. In meekness instructing those who oppose themselves." That more and better battles for the Lord are won by love than by wrath.

If I have been successful in my ministry in quelling strifes, I owe much of my success under God to what I learned semi-unconsciously here.

Again sitting under the preaching of a sound gospel; thoroughly orthodox and yet not timid of new truth.

Listening to the reasonings of men, but never letting go of those "Thus saith the Lords"—how often do I recall his emphasizing these—I have never lost my love for the old truths, nor grown too big for the Bible of my fathers.

No one can fully tell the effects of the plain, simple preaching of the truth.

I attribute also somewhat of my love and interest in the circulating of the Scriptures to what I learned here as in a sort of religious kindergarten.

Well do I recall those annual offerings for the County Bible Society. When after the appeal to the importance of the work had been made, the subscriptions were taken and one, two, three at least, some years perhaps more, names had set opposite them $30 for a life membership. From year to year this was repeated until there were families in which the husband and the wife and each of the children became L. M.'s of the Bible Society in this way.

Do you wonder that such scenes left their impress? And that when I in turn asked my people to contribute to the Bible cause I could do so with ease and confidence and generally with marked success?

Here, too, I learned my first lessons about the heathen without the gospel. And as this church was never tardy in its sympathy and loving gifts for the outcast and the lost of earth in the regions beyond, I caught the lesson early in life that my Christian love must be worldwide.

Those early impressions have never left me.

The importance of an education was impressed upon me here. A small village is not the easiest place to obtain this. And yet I recall that when good old Dr. Campbell, President of Rutgers College, came here seeking for friends to aid in the indorsement of that institution, he found some who were willing to give the amount of a scholarship in the hope that one or more of their sons would desire to enjoy a collegiate education.

There has been a long line of college graduates from this church. The pastor of this church for forty-two years believed, and he often emphasized his conviction that every lad desirous of a college education ought to be sent. Possibly some of us, sons of this church in the ministry and elsewhere in useful callings, never will know exactly all the influence he exerted to open the way for our higher education.

Finally there is one other influence for good received here of which I wished to speak. We hear much of C. E. in these latter days, and well it is. But there was a Christian Endeavor in this congregation before modern C. E. ever shaped itself into existence, which has helped me to this hour.

About twenty-seven years ago in one of the homes of this congregation, half a dozen or more young men met to open their lips for the first time in public prayer. I was one of them. I see some of them now before me. Some have gone on into the heavens. But there we fought our battle against timidity and self-distrust and gained a mastery for life.

But more than that, I learned a lesson of sympathy for the young, and felt a desire to aid such, where I had needed help, which has never left me.

And I can say with pride and joy and conscious success that I

REV. B. V. D. WYCKOFF,
PRESENT PASTOR, 1894.

have never been the pastor of a church for a single year in these, my nineteen years of service for Christ, without having a young people's prayer meeting service.

Such are a few of the things which impress me as I stand up to-night and wish my old mother church a word of joy and Godspeed for her beneficial influences bestowed upon me as she celebrates her century and three-quarters birthday. May she live to round out her second century, and many, many centuries of years of usefulness.

Address of the Rev. Gilbert Lane.

Rev. Gilbert Lane, the oldest of the ministerial children of Readington Church, said as follows, as near as he could recall it: He expressed his great gratification in being permitted to enjoy and participate in the exercises of this memorable occasion and while feeling young was convinced that he could not be young (as measured by years), for it was forty years (40), ago that the Classis of Philadelphia, to which this church then belonged, met in this place to examine him for license, and that not only the venerable Dr. Labaugh, who signed his license with feeble and trembling hand, but all the other ministers of the Classis, who then ministered in the several congregations, have ceased from labor and been called to enjoy the reward of the faithful. He thought it becoming in this gathering of the ministerial children of the congregation to say a word about those who preceded him in the ministry, with whom he had enjoyed acquaintanceship.

The first was the Rev. Peter O. Studdiford, licensed in 1821, and who labored for the Master in the Presbyterian Church of Lambertville, N. J., of whom he says:

It was during the last years of his life that I enjoyed this acquaintance with him. I admired him for his learning, ability and eloquence, but I learned to love him, for his piety, his sympathy and the encouragement he gave to me as a young and diffident brother. He labored long, faithfully and successfully.

The next son of the church was the Rev. Cornelius Wyckoff, licensed in 1838. I visited him when I was a student. This visit was not only pleasant, but instructive, and I held him in great esteem as long as he lived. I have never forgotten a remark he made about his very large congregation of 300 families in Ulster County, N. Y., the present pastor of which is the Rev. John L. McNair. He divided the congregation in three parts; 100 families were regular church attendants, 100 families occasional, and the other 100 never. Their desire for and need of a minister did not extend beyond their desire that he should marry them, and preach a funeral sermon when they died. I relate this experience with the hope that Bro. Wyckoff, of Readington, will never have to make this division or anything like it in his congregation.

The next minister licensed from this congregation was the Rev. Wm. J. Thompson, in 1841. He labored for three years in the pastorate, and then entered on the great work of his life, the preparing students for college and business life; and in Rutgers College Grammar School, and other places made his mark as an able and successful instructor, as I with many others can testify, and are thankful now, if we were not always then, for the severe drilling that he gave us, in the laying of a good foundation for a liberal education. It can be said of him (in the best and truest sense), "he rests from his labors and his works do follow him."

The Rev. John Simonson, the ministerial brother next preceding me, was licensed in 1845. Before this he for some time taught the village school in Readington, which I attended in my boyhood. I seldom met him afterward, but I know from the church records that he labored for the Master, in the churches of

Bethlehem, West Farms and Plainfield. The Great Shepherd has lately called him to his eternal reward.

In view of the limited time necessarily awarded to each speaker, on account of the size of this church's ministerial family, I am glad that I feel like the candidate for the office of *Auditor*, whom I once heard in North Carolina at the Hustings, where all who had been nominated for office, were expected to appear and advocate their claim to office. When he was called upon for a speech he rose up and said: "I do not want to be a Speaker, I want to be an auditor."

Closing now before the time limit, thus affording those to follow me more time, I think I also comply with an Apostolic injunction that says: "In honor preferring one another."

Address of the Rev. Herman Hageman.

A boy always has a warm place in his heart for his mother. Of all the persons living or dead, he cannot hear her name spoken against, for she does more in moulding his character than any one else. Daniel Webster often alluded to his mother, and the way he referred to her was this: "My honored mother." Abraham Lincoln, though his mother died when he was but 10 years old, said: "All that I am I owe to my mother." Some one has said if you would reform a man, you must be present and pick out his grandfather and his grandmother. We are not able to do this, and so the work of reform goes on but slowly.

Now, though I had nothing to do with the selection of my grandparents, or my parents, I am very grateful to Almighty God he gave me the ones he did. I am also very thankful I was born in the place where I was. I am glad of the hayseeds which used to get on me, and I trust I shall never want to lose the recollection of them. And especially to-night am I glad that God permitted me to have this honored church as my church home. Had I my own selection I would choose to-day this church to begin my Christian life as I remember the church of my childhood. Now, when we boys are asked to come home and to give in just ten minutes an expression of our appreciation of the worth of our church mother, the idea is simply preposterous. We ought to have at least seven days to tell of our love for the old church home and of our appreciation of what she has done for us.

Now there are a great many things I have forgotten that transpired when I was a boy. A good many things no doubt the majority of you have forgotten. There are some things that I recall that I trust you have likewise forgotten.

But there are certain things which have left an indelible impression on my mind, for which I thank God even to-day. David was at one time sorely pressed by his enemies, and it seemed to him as though he might die and at this moment he made this request: "Oh, that one would give me to drink of the water of the Well of Bethlehem, which is by the gate." The very taste of the water in the well around which he had played in childhood had made its impression, and in an hour of danger he longed for a drink from that very well. How often in my experience as a minister have the scenes of boyhood days come to mind, and I have, like David, longed to drink from the spiritual well of my childhood. Some bygone scenes may be a little rosy-tinted as seen through the distance of intervening years, yet there are times when the old scenes of life are most satisfactory. Now one thing about this old church that made an indelible impression on my mind, and for which I have often longed, was the attendance on divine service. The early years of my churchgoing were years when every one went to church. Who can ever forget the scenes of those Sabbath days? The long string of wagons coming to the church, or the scenes in front of the church—like it was to-day, or the scene as they formed in line and drove from the church? Yes, some one says, they came early and gossipped a great deal before the service began. Yes, perhaps they did, but before they went home they heard the pure, simple gospel proclaimed by the pastor of my boyhood, and the records of the church show how many were converted under his plain and practical preaching.

The people did not work on Sunday. Their practice was to come to church. I recall one case, however, where a man carted in his hay on the Sabbath, and in two weeks' time his barns burned. And to my boyish mind, as I looked on the burning building, I regarded it as cause and effect. Superstition you say. Perhaps, but God give us a little more superstition if that is the word to use concerning the fact that God's judgments follow a violation of his laws. In those days we were free from the influence of the Sunday newspaper and the flashy, trashy literature of to-day, which is unfitting so many for the attendance upon and a participation in the worship of God's house. And when we to-day see so many who are neglecting the Sabbath, and even trying to destroy it, may we not be pardoned if at times as the scenes of boyhood days come to mind we long for a drink from the water of the well of Bethlehem which is by the gate?

This church also stands in my memory as one that had implicit faith in the Bible and in the doctrines of the church. This people regarded the Bible as the Word of God. They received it with childlike faith. It was handed down from one generation to another as the Word of God. This fact is explained by the character of the men who proclaimed the Word of God. This pulpit has never had in it a man who was weak-kneed concerning the Word of God. Of the nine preachers there has never been an unsound one in all the number. And one result has been that this people regard the Bible as the Word of God. The Heidelbergh Catechism was preached and taught. The class in the northeast corner of the basement were expected to learn it, though they often discouraged the heart of their teacher. At the present time and during recent years we have heard a great deal about the mistakes of the Bible. Higher criticism has weakened the faith of many in the Word of God. One has tried to show the mistakes of Moses, and science and learning have proven the mistakes to be those of the other party. Yet with a great many their faith in the Word of God has been lessened. Now this may explain the longing one sometimes has for the good old days when the Bible had a power over the heart and life. The water in the well of childhood days we long for because it was a pure, unadulterated gospel.

Still one other fact comes to mind concerning this mother church which sometimes creates a longing for old scenes, viz.: The character of the men and women who composed the working force of this church. As a boy I always had the greatest admiration for their sterling worth. There were those who like Saul stood head and shoulders above the rest of the people. They were Christians through and through. There was no questioning about their religion. Their lives—their faces showed it. Many of them have gone home triumphant in the gospel. They are a part of the cloud of witnesses watching us to-day. A few of these older ones remain to bear the burdens a little while longer and then to enter upon their rest and reward. This church may well thank God for these Christians of such sterling worth. They showed it in their their daily work. They showed it in their attendance at the prayer meeting. They showed it in their contributions. Their consecration was as another has said "coinsecration," They were converted, pocketbook and all. They showed it in their families. As Dr. Campbell once said, "I love to think that grace when it once enters a family never dies out." So there are here many families where the work of grace has gone on, generation after generation the sons of the church come from godly homes. In all thank God that He has blessed us with pious, sanctified parents. There are these godly lines which have given this church a peculiar, fascinating charm. They have made this church what it has been, a power and a blessing. And to many of these the words have been spoken, " Well done, good and faithful servant, enter thou into the joy of thy Lord."

And now a thought in closing. The work of the church goes on, and ought to go on grandly. A glorious legacy has been left you, even those things we held dear and precious. Now your lives ought to be broader and more energetic than ever your fathers' were. For you start life, not where your fathers began, but where they left off. "Instead of the fathers shall be the children." Unless the work of the fathers has been a failure, you are to labor where they laid the work aside. Therefore let every one do his best in his day and generation.

I pray God that he will so qualify you all that the next twenty-five years of this church's history shall be the grandest of all the grand years of the past, and when we come to celebrate the close of the second century of her existence—for which time God spare our lives—may we be able to say that the years that intervene between then and now have been the grandest years of all.

Address of the Rev. Elias W. Thompson.

It is right a son or daughter should come to the mother once in a while, and tell of the love they have for her who bore them. It is still more fitting that a baby boy, provided he can talk, should come and tell his mother how glad he is to hear others speak well of her, especially when he has always thought her to be the very best mother in all the world. As the youngest son of this church, I want to add my congratulations to those already offered, and say that I am proud that it *is my* mother church whose history is so grand, and whose influence is so wide.

A prominent author of modern days has written that there are some old places which are destined to be forever new. True it is that the more we study about old places and things, the more there is yet to learn about them. Time brings to old age an ever-increasing and everlasting novelty. Of Readington, to-day this is doubly true. "Poor old Readington" in New Jersey has now become New Readington in Old Jersey. We have heard of her past achievements; of her relations with her sister churches that call her their mother. What about her future?

Tennyson writes in the opening verses of "In Memoriam":

> "I held it truth with him who sings
> To one clear harp in divers tones,
> That men may rise on stepping-stones
> Of their dead selves, to better things.
> But who shall so forecast the years
> And find in loss a gain to match,
> Or reach a hand through time to catch
> The far off interest of tears."

Shall we now rise to better things on the stepping stones of the past? The history of the fathers who are now no more shows us that the past had its losses. Is there in the influence they have exerted, and in that which we can exert, a gain to match? The past is gone. Present opportunities are now ours. By attending well to these do we make the future safe? Am I to be the last of the ministerial sons of this church? So far as I know, there is now no member of this church who has the ministry in view. Are there no parents who would call it the highest honor to have their sons in the ministry? Fathers and mothers, are you training your children to make the preachers of the future? As ye present your babes in baptism do ye consecrate them to the Lord, and bring them up with this in view. I once heard one of the leading preachers in our church say that the theology of the future was dependent upon the influence of the mothers who are now teaching their boys to pray at the knee. Is there not much that we can do along this very line? As we love this church, let us do all we can to widen her influence. It can be done in no better way than by making her through her sons a glory not only to the community, but also to the denomination, and above all, through these to the great head of the church. May we all be awakened to a new life, and may the mantle of the fathers fall upon the sons, who in true devotion shall ever sing of this church here,

> "For her my tears shall fall,
> For her my prayers ascend.
> To her my cares and toils be given
> Till toils and cares shall end."

Address of the Rev. Jacob A. Craig.

Brothers and Sisters:—It gives me great pleasure to be present at this anniversary, and be permitted to look into the faces of so many of my former companions and acquaintances and friends on this 175th anniversary of the Readington Church.

It occurs to me that you have left this church a long time without an anniversary. If we as a Nation had left the celebrating of our National Independence for 175 years, we should have little to celebrate now. I do not come to represent one of the ministerial sons of the church, for at my conversion I cast my fortunes with the Methodist Episcopal Church, and while my father and two brothers are members of this to-day, we are still brethren and striving for the Kingdom. I came rather to bear you the greetings and congratulations of a sister denomination, who much younger in years than your church, yet has to-day over a million communicants that gather at her altar. We have blazed our way through forest and plain, until to-day there is scarcely a land that the sun shines upon where the stirring hymns and prayers, and exhortations are not heard, urging the people to repentance and faith in our Lord Jesus Christ. I am proud to belong to a church that is to-day raising twelve hundred thousand dollars to spread the gospel throughout the world.

If the exact number could be ascertained throughout the land it would reveal the fact that thousands upon thousands who have passed over the river, and thousands more here on earth date their conversion to the faithful and earnest preaching of the gospel as proclaimed by Methodist preachers. I do not say it boastingly, but to the glory of God. God speed you, in the work of lifting up the cross of Jesus, and when we shall strike glad hands on the other shore. We'll give all the glory to him who has redeemed us with his own precious blood.

At the conclusion of these admirable addresses the pastor stated that while Readington was proud of her many sons in the ministry, she had also some sons who had chosen the law as their profession in whom she was exceedingly interested. One such he would introduce as the closing speaker, John L. Connet, Esq., of Flemington.

Address of J. L. Connet, Esq.

As the years go flitting by so rapidly that we can scarcely take note or keep account of them, we are all engrossed in our various avocations, seeking to advance ourselves in knowledge, or else to secure for ourselves and those who shall come after us a competency of this world's goods, and this is right, so long as it is not done to the exclusion of a greater good. But aside from our business, and the duties to which we devote our lives and our strength, our time and our energies, it seems to me there are three things which go to make up in large measure the sum of human existence: The associations and attachments we form in this life, those memories we cherish of the past, and the hopes we build for the future; whether of this life, or that greater life which knows no ending.

Unconsciously, perhaps, the lives of others, and sometimes inanimate things grow into our own lives before we are aware, and the severance of them seems like taking away a part of our own persons. Even a favorite horse or dog gets a hold upon our affections oftentimes, which it is hard to break, and we know that when a friend dies or parts from us, a thread is broken, and a blank comes into our lives, so that we are never again quite as we were before. So, I have always had a strong attachment for this people and this church. And why should it not be so? It was here that my feet first trod the sanctuary, and it was here that I first heard from the sacred desk the words of eternal life. 'Tis true I was young, and could not comprehend the full import and meaning of those words so well as in later years, but the seed was sown, and what the harvest shall be, eternity alone can reveal.

Sabbath after Sabbath my brother brought me with him to this sanctuary.

It was here that I received the first lessons in spiritual things; and even after I left here I was not wholly severed from this congregation, for after a few years my lot was cast with Rev. Henry P. Thompson, with whom I lived for three years. He was also a son of this church. And it was in his church, also of the same denomination as this, that I first publicly avowed my allegiance to the Lord Jesus Christ.

Then, too, in the church I now attend there has been and still is a number of persons, who are children of this same church. So you see the association has never been entirely broken. And when

I look over these seats and call to mind the faces that used to be here, and think of the friends of my boyhood days, and remember that now so many of them are in that land whose shores are washed by the river of Life, the thoughts grow tender and the attachment becomes the stronger.

Then, again, my heart is united to your interests because in "the low green tents" on yonder hillside, where the morning sun kisses the verdant mounds, and the nightly dews fall gently on them, sleeps the sacred dust of my little brother and sister, and of my venerable father, awaiting the resurrection morn. How can the attachment ever be broken?

And recollection is busy to-night. Back over all the years that lie between runs the memory and links the past with the present. Memory is like an electric cable, and connects the empire of yesterday with the empire of to-day.

Again I see myself in the old schoolhouse over there, conning the lessons of the hour, waiting so anxiously for the noon spell to come when I could play knife, tag or ball, or dabble with bare feet in the cooling waters of the brook.

Unless you have had personal experience yourself you cannot understand and appreciate the keen, the very keen recollections I have of attendance in that old school house.

Why, although years have rolled away, and passed into the oblivion of the gone forever, so far as human knowledge goes, and one would think that the passing years and the changes made by time, would blot those scenes from one's memory, yet it seems to me that sometimes 1 can feel the sting of the master's rod still. Yes, those recollections are keen.

But 'tis not of these things that I am thinking most now, but it is of this church. If there is any one thing of my earlier years that I remember with greater distinctness than another, it is my attendance upon the service and Sabbath School of this sanctuary.

From my earliest infancy I might say, my mother brought me here to church. Don't I remember the cakes she used to bring with her, with which to keep me quiet, when the sermon was too long for my non-comprehensive mind? How I call to mind how she used to find the text, and when she had read it, pass the book to me. I would follow it with the minister as he repeated it, but then when he went on to preach, I could not find the rest in the scripture, and got lost in a maze of uncertainty.

Dr. Van Liew was the first, and for a long time the only minister I ever knew. I saw him almost every day, for he often came to my father's house to talk politics or something else, and I thought him one of the best men who ever lived, as he most assuredly was.

I was a boy and I did not know all the good people of the congregation very well, nor did I know just how good it was necessary for one to be to entitle him to a place in Heaven. The impression I had was that one had to be very, very good, and for a long time, I knew of only two persons who I thought were absolutely sure of a home in the realms of eternal bliss. I was not one of them. They were Dr. Van Liew and George Washington; Washington, because he never told a lie, and Mr. Van Liew, because he was so absolutely good. I supposed there were others, but I did not know them, and I thought I would rather go with the larger crowd.

Dr. Van Liew's pastorate was an exceedingly long one, and one blessed of God. I doubt not that many of you sat under his ministry. He baptized you in your infancy, married you in your young manhood and womanhood, and at the soul's new birth, received you into the communion of this church; and when the shadows fell, he officiated at the burial of your dead. Thus the memories of the past come trooping up, and to me those memories are precious and sweet, though touched perhaps with a tinge of sadness, when we see how far we are drifting away from our earlier years. But—

> "When time, which steals our years away,
> Shall steal our pleasures, too,
> The memory of the past will stay,
> And half our joy renew."

For a century and three-quarters, this church has been as a fountain of living water to thousands who have had the privilege of drinking therefrom ; the truths taught, the promises repeated, and the instructions given, have been the means of giving a hope of eternal life to those who have heard them. Wide has been the scope of her power and influence, and to her many daughters have been born. From her have been sent out more young persons to proclaim the gospel of the Son of God to a lost and ruined world, than from any other congregation of its size of which I have any knowledge.

Proud is her prestige and great her power for good.

All of her pastors, some of whom are known to me, Van Liew, Van Slyke, Smock, and the present pastor, have been earnest, devoted workers, and lovers of the souls of men. Short as has been the pastorate of the present guardian of this flock, he has endeared himself to his people, and great good has been accomplished by him.

And as we stand upon this dividing line between the past and the future, it seems to me that the years of success which he has had here, are but a brief foretaste of what God will vouchsafe to him in the years that lie ahead. He has many things upon which he can congratulate himself and for which he is to be congratulated. He is a vessel chosen of God for good. His past is fraught with the consciousness of duties faithfully performed, and of souls saved through his labors. And his surroundings are full of encouragement and promise for the future. He is young and full of hope, and by his side stand many ready and willing to give him a helping hand. The older members are strong and conservative. The youth are active and enthusiastic. In the Young People's Society of Christian Endeavor he has a most powerful auxiliary. And surrounded and supported by them, he travels down the Christian pathway, a pathway illumined by the radiance that streams from Calvary, and the gems that shall adorn his diadem, will be the souls that through his ministry, have found and will find "the peace of God that passeth understanding."

After Mr. Connet's address hymn 375 was announced and sung, the congregation standing. At its conclusion the Rev. A. J. Hageman, of Somerville, offered a brief prayer and pronounced the benediction.

List of Relics and Antiquities
on Exhibition at the Anniversary.

There was an interesting collection of "antiquities" on exhibition. A portfolio prepared for the occasion contained pictures of the various church edifices, with diagrams of pews, prices, etc. There were bills of sale for slaves and their effects, receipts for subscriptions to *The Federalist*, receipted bills of doctors of the last century, autographs of the early Frelinghuysens, and one of Caspar Wistar, who founded the first glasshouse in New Jersey. There were several autograph papers of the Revolutionary patriot, Abraham Post (the nephew of Theunis Post, the official "helper" of the first pastor); as well as of his son, Henry, the elder who carried Domine Studdiford into the church that he might preach the last sermon before he died; and of *his* son, John, the elder whom the

Lord sent (as a missionary *without the name*) to build up churches at Oakfield, N. Y., at Raritan, Ill., and at Somerset, Kan. There was the big Dutch Bible of Altje Blauw, and the Testament and Psalms of Antje Aten, both of them with family records of the last century. There were the family records of Lucas Schermorn and Willempje Voorhees (*nee* Wyckoff) which genealogists have been so long looking for in vain. There was the Bible and family record of the Scotch John Thomson, who "was killed and scalped by ye Tory and Indians at Shomokem," with the commissions of his son and grandsons as judges of the County Courts, signed by various governors of the state. There was the roster of a military company of the early years of the century, with the commissions of its officers, and what remains of the flag they carried at general training. There was a picture of the village and of the man who painted it in 1847. There were girlish letters that passed between girls whose grandchildren and great-grandchildren are now ministers of the gospel of mature age. There was a " Breeches' Bible" with the autograph of "John Cole" and other owners. There was a copy of the treatise on language by Erasmus of Rotterdam, printed in 1523, with an appended letter of his to his father, and an edition of the letters of the younger Pliny, printed at Venice in 1501. The docket of Esquire Ezekiel Cole, and the day-book of the man who kept "the still" a hundred years ago, were full of interest. There were antique canes once carried by ancient members of the church; and wooden shoes worn by Hollanders of more recent immigration.

Most interesting of all were the ancient records of the church itself, which, we trust, will soon be carefully rebound and placed in the fireproof library at New Brunswick.

It deserves to be added here that much is due to the patience and laborious effort of the Rev. J. B. Thompson, D. D., for the fullness of this list.

We would also here express our gratitude to him for many suggestions given in the preparation of the program.

Letter of Prof. H. A. Scomp.

PARKSVILLE, KY., OCT. 11, 1894. MR. AARON THOMPSON, READINGTON, N. J. *My Dear Sir:*—I have just received a copy of the invitation to the 175th anniversary of the founding of Old Readington Church. I wish to express my appreciation of this beautiful reminder that I am still considered a child of the dear old house where my fathers worshipped.

From that tabernacle set up in the wilderness the incense has been wafted by a thousand breezes—a savour of sweet odors for altars in far distant lands. Its members have gone forth as pioneers to the wilds of the West; they have carried with them the sacred fire and the Penates of the old household. In them have been kept alive the devotion, the zeal and the simple faith of Huguenots and Walloons, who, for religion's sake, sought refuge long ago in the Netherlands. They, along with the sturdy Hollanders, fought the battles of freedom of conscience and freedom of worship against the tyranny of Spain, the treachery of Valois and Bourbon, and the craft and malice of Italy) How much the world of religious thought owes to Holland ! How much do the great principles of political freedom owe to that religious creed which tolerated neither Pope nor Bishop; which recognized *one* Lord and Master, but none else beside !

With them the Book was the final court of appeal in all matters of conscience and duty. Absolutism can never live in the presence of such a creed. It is not wonderful that such men were patriots in the Revolution ; they could stand nowhere else. It is noteworthy that their migrations were so commonly congregational in character. Whole communities removed together, carrying their pastors with them. The wilderness shut in their humble camps when night or the Sabbath arrested their wanderings and the wild forests re-echoed their songs and prayers. They pitched their habitations together and perpetuated in the names of their new churches and in the mountains and forest streams the memories of their fatherland. Naught but the bond of a common faith can cement such a brotherhood. It was like the exodus of Israel, or the return of the captivity from Babylon. It was such as the simple faith of the Acadians, out of which grew the beautiful story of Evangeline. Such strong faith has ever been the nucleus for organizing a government of peace and justice among men. May we be worthy of our sires and able to transmit uncorrupted the principles they have bequeathed to us.

How much I should like to be with you on that auspicious anniversary; but circumstances will prevent my coming. I expect to return to Georgia next week. May the occasion prove to be all that the most sanguine could hope for; and may all of old Readington's children in the gospel, far and nigh, do honor to the venerable mother from whose body they sprung.

Yours, sincerely,

H. A. Scomp.

ADDENDUM TO NOTE ON PAGE 16.

Since going to press with the earlier portion of this book it has been ascertained that the date of the burning of the church in 1864 *was* March 24—not March 22. A newspaper clipping in the possession of John Fleming, of Readington, together with a minute of the event in the church record book, fully establish this fact.

www.ingramcontent.com/pod-product-compliance
Lightning Source LLC
Chambersburg PA
CBHW031118160426
43192CB00008B/1037